"This is an unexpected treasure—a gift found when you weren't even looking. Dr. Schultze's wisdom connects with readers; his stories paint pictures that make his experience their own."

—Linda W. Belton, FACHE; author of *A Nobler Side of Leadership: The Art of Humanagement*

"This marvelous little book will put you on the road to becoming a wiser and more winsome leader. Begin your 30-day journey today."

—Dr. Tim Muehlhoff, Professor of Communication, Biola University; author of *I Beg to Differ* and *Winsome Persuasion*

"Wow! Compelling, relevant, personal stories about how anyone who wants to lead can communicate with purpose and integrity. This terrific book is now my personal reading for professional growth."

—Christopher VanOosterhout, web entrepreneur and Professor of Business, Muskegon Community College

"Whether a newcomer or a seasoned traveler, you will find this book to be one you go back to time and again for insights and encouragement. Robert Greenleaf would have been proud to have this book at his side."

—Dr. Mary Meehan, President Emeritus, Alverno College

"Quentin Schultze understands that words are a leader's most important tools, and in his clear and engaging prose he not only teaches the art of servant leadership but demonstrates the power of those tools. There have been many leadership books that have taught us less with many more words. This collection of succinct, honest, self-revealing stories teaches us not only about leadership but about life itself."

—James A. Autry, former CEO of Meredith Corporation's magazine group; author of *Love & Profit* and *The Servant Leader*

"Dr. Schultze has the heart and motivation of a servant leader. This book belongs on everyone's iPad or shelf. In 30 days, after reading the book and making a few notes, you will likely discover how this little book is transforming your life."

—**Richard R. Pieper, Sr.**, Non-Executive Chairman, PPC Partners, Inc.

"This splendid book defies categorization; it's equal parts personal narrative, practical guidance, and leadership inspiration. Quentin's lifetime of communication wisdom shines through on every page."

—**Gary Van Prooyen**, VP Marketing & Communications, ISACA; Former Sr. Director, Global Brand, Motorola

"I highly recommend this book to anyone who aspires to be a servant leader. You'll see why Quentin is in demand on campus and in the boardroom. Every chapter challenged me to step up my leadership presence."

—**Skip Prichard**, President & CEO, OCLC; author of *The Book of Mistakes*; writer of the "Leadership Insights" blog at skipprichard.com

"Dr. Schultze masterfully takes the writings and wisdom of Robert Greenleaf on servant leadership and weaves a tapestry of communication insights and practices for anyone seeking to enhance their leadership. If you're looking for a guide to become a servant leader communicator, this book is a must-read."

—**Dr. Kathryn Scanland**, Principal, Greystone Global LLC

"Vitally practical and virtue-focused, this book engages the heart and mind. It challenges us to reflect and grow into better servant leaders."

—**Dr. Annalee R. Ward**, Director, Wendt Character Initiative, University of Dubuque

"This book is in a class by itself. It will actually help you become a better, wiser, happier leader."

—**Dr. Richard C. Wallace**, Professor Emeritus and Dean, Gainey School of Business, Spring Arbor University

"This short, easy-to-read book is filled with wisdom and sits at the front of my desk. If you want to grow as a leader-communicator, buy, read, and apply this book."

—**Dr. Chris Hamstra**, Associate Professor of English and Communication, Davenport University

"Quentin displays a keen understanding of servant leadership, and applies its principles to effective communication with a light, humorous, and effective touch. Readers of Greenleaf who are looking for guidance on how to effectively persuade, motivate, and lead will find this insightful."

—**Dr. G. James Lemoine**, Assistant Professor, Organization and Human Resources, School of Management, University at Buffalo

"Writing with a warm and generous heart, Dr. Schultze makes a substantial contribution to all leaders and communicators who take the time to linger over these meditations."

—**Dr. John Pauley**, Vice Provost for Academic Affairs; Dean of the College of Arts and Sciences, Eastern University

"Shakespeare wrote, 'To thine own self be true.' Quentin Schultze summarizes in 30 eloquent daily readings how important it is for servant leaders to find internal peace through honest introspection. Anyone who has the honor of leading should reflect each day on his lessons. A true leader is such only by the grace of those who willingly follow."

—**H. Dale Hall**, CEO, Ducks Unlimited Inc.; Director, U.S. Fish and Wildlife Service (Retired)

"Quentin has an impressive approach of connecting great content with great reflective questions to help the reader grow in self-awareness. This is a powerful approach for building credible communicators and leaders."

—Joseph M. Patrnchak, Principal Green Summit Partners; author of *The Engaged Enterprise: A Field Guide for the Servant Leader*

"This is a unique book in format and content—a wonderful way for a leader to continue to evaluate important requirements for developing as a real leader-communicator. There is much wisdom in this small book. Schultze is a sought-out mentor and this book is a wonderful tutorial for all mentors and mentees."

—Chaplain (Colonel) Herman Keizer, Jr., US Army (retired)

"*Communicate Like a True Leader* is a wonderful 'daily meditation' for anyone aspiring to a life of Servant Leadership."

—Larry Gluth, President & CEO, Bobby Dodd Institute; Chair of the Governance Committee for the Greenleaf Center for Servant Leadership

"Again, Dr. Schultze imparts his thoughtful wisdom that meets me exactly where I am on life's path. I keep this book close by as a reference tool for effective and wise communication with friends, colleagues, and family."

—Andrea Rip, Marketing Manager, Abu Dhabi

"I savored each meditation and found them to be challenging, humbling, thought provoking, wise, and immediately helpful in many of my life and leadership roles. I plan to read them often as I've found the lessons are even richer the second and third times around. I recommend this book to all who are serious about becoming better communicators, better servant leaders, and even better human beings."

—Dr. Robert H. Eames, Professor of Business, and Director, Calvin Center for Innovation in Business, Calvin College; consultant; investor

"We all stand to improve our abilities to lead and serve others. With keen insight, experience, and humor, Dr. Schultze has written a masterful, concise guide for turning servant leadership concepts into everyday practices. When this book finds its way into the hands and hearts of readers, leadership will become less about administering authority than stewarding and celebrating the gifts all around us."

—Dr. Don Waisanen, Assoc. Professor of Communication, Austin W. Marxe School of Public and International Affairs, Baruch College, CUNY

"Dr. Schultze has always had keen insights into communication. His latest book takes us into the history of his life, candidly showing us what molded his ability to communicate wisely and well."

Holly Yavanian, Sr. Project Manager & Business Analyst, Mirum Agency

"Dr. Schultze's new book allows us to explore various ingredients of servant leadership and, like a wonderful meal, savor each bite until it becomes part of our being. This is a valuable resource for those of us seeking to integrate the philosophy of servant leadership into our lives."

—Dr. Robert Thomas, Professor of the Practice, Director of Leadership Education, Scheller College of Business, Georgia Tech

"Every emerging young leader should engage with this quick read early in their leadership journey (as should seasoned leaders already well along)."

—John Scroggins, Executive Director, The Baton Exchange

"This book brings fresh ideas and distills old wisdom about what we say, how we say it, and when we say it. It prompts us to think about important things like mentorship and friendship, legacy and listening."

—Shirley Hoogstra, President, Council for Christian Colleges & Universities

Selected Books by Quentin J. Schultze

An Essential Guide to Interpersonal Communication: Building Great Relationships with Faith, Skill, and Virtue
(with Diane M. Badzinski)

Résumé 101: A Student and Recent Grad Guide to Crafting Résumés and Cover Letters that Land Jobs

An Essential Guide to Public Speaking: Serving Your Audience with Faith, Skill, and Virtue

Habits of the High-Tech Heart: Living Virtuously in the Information Age

Communicate Like a True Leader

30 Days of Life-Changing Wisdom

Quentin J. Schultze

Foreword by
Leonard Sweet

Edenridge Press LLC
Grand Rapids, Michigan

Copyright © 2017 by Quentin J. Schultze

Published by
Edenridge Press LLC
Grand Rapids, Michigan USA
service@edenridgepress.com

Quantity discount pricing is available.
service@edenridgepress.com

Edited by Robert Banning, Turning Leaves Editorial.
Cover Design by Matthew Plescher.

Schultze, Quentin J.
communicate like a true leader: 30 days of life-changing
wisdom / Quentin J. Schultze ; foreword by Leonard
Sweet

ISBN-10 193753281X
ISBN-13 978-1-937532-81-9 (alk. Paper)
LCCN: 2017911060

BUS 071000 BUSINESS & ECONOMICS /
Leadership

Printed in the United States of America

Dedication

To the memory of Robert K. Greenleaf, whose spirit lives in the wisdom we servant leaders continue to ponder and employ. May this book serve as a worthy jazz performance based on the themes of Greenleaf's work.

And to Max DePree, a gifted soul who helped me listen to the voices of wisdom, judgment, and the common good.

Acknowledgments

My debts are so broad and deep that I hardly know where to begin. So I would like to sketch some contours and simply apologize to the many additional individuals whose words and lives have provided me with the personal and professional tutelage that I needed in order to write this book.

For over three decades I taught communication courses at Calvin College in Grand Rapids, Michigan. The wonderful students at that fine school taught me how to teach, mentor, and ultimately lead through example with skill and virtue. Many of them became my long-term mentees and continue to teach me through the personal and professional challenges that they courageously share with me. They have assumed that I have been giving them advice, but their lives have been case studies for my own instruction as a leader and even as a human being. Among them are Stacey Wieland, Kevin Schut, Art Bamford, Rick DeVos, Brad Van Arragon, Sara Toering, and Chris Hamstra.

I'm deeply grateful for a plethora of consulting opportunities. Many of these projects were highly confidential involving leadership crises, institutional breakdowns, and complicated business situations. I served as an outside reviewer for many leaders and organizations. I walked with leaders through their personal and professional problems. I learned more about leadership and communication through these experiences than any other activities in my life. I discovered that many high-placed leaders simply lack friends. They need people whom they can deeply trust and to whom they can confide some of their deepest fears and most confounding issues, the bulk of which involve communication.

One of the most important people in whom I could confide was Rev. Arthur H. DeKruyter, founding pastor of Christ Church of Oak Brook, Illinois. I discovered in Art the rare servant leader who could simultaneously be deeply self-critical and spaciously encouraging. There was nothing that Art and I couldn't discuss about communication and leadership in our own lives. He became not only a mentor, but also a friend. Yet he would come to me for advice even though I had relatively meager life experience. I learned from Art how to honor those who live with deep self doubts—simply by listening to them, affirming them, and encouraging them. I was deeply honored at Calvin College to hold the Arthur H. DeKruyter Chair in Faith and Communication.

One of my most inspiring activities over the years was to advise Gospel Communications International (GCI), which served a broad consortium of ministries. Led by a visionary board headed by Rich DeVos, and a company leadership team driven by the brilliant and highly idiosyncratic Billy Zeoli, GCI gave me a platform to try out many of the communication principles in this book. Eventually Doug DeVos chaired the board, and through a related foundation provided seed funding for me to work on various projects, including this book. My debts to Rich, Billy, and Doug are considerable. I'm grateful for their trust in me.

This will sound strange, but I need to acknowledge someone who protected me from leadership positions. The long-term chair of my department at Calvin College, Randall Bytwerk, worked hard to keep me from being pulled into academic leadership over many years. He realized that I could best serve the college and other organizations as a kind of freelance leader rather than as a more internal, managerial one. In this book I use Max DePree's term "roving leader" to describe the remarkable freedom I had as a roving professor. Randy also talked me out of pursuing leadership positions that would have stymied my entrepreneurial instincts. He has been a gem of colleague and friend.

I learned to write both by doing it and by learning from terrific editors. Bob Banning of Turning Leaves Editorial taught me as much about writing as anyone else. He became the kind of editor who knew better than I did what exactly I was trying to say. Whenever possible, I have worked with Bob on writing projects. This book is one example. It would not be nearly as winsome, cogent, and lucid without Bob's extraordinary editorial abilities.

As my book dedication indicates, I am deeply grateful to Robert Greenleaf and Max DePree. Their work and lives have inspired me to be a servant leader. I consider them gifts.

I could express thanks to many family members who serve me abundantly, but I would like to highlight one person who is not even reading yet. My grandson Elliot and I have been spending time together a couple of days a week. One day, while shuttling between caring for him and writing, I realized how important his playfulness has been for my thinking and writing. His friendship has helped to keep me from taking myself too seriously. It has also kept me asking myself the "why" questions that are so important in both leadership and communication. He asks "why" about nearly everything. "Elliot, let's go to the store." "Why?" "Elliot, shall we have lunch?" "Why?" "Elliot, I think it's time for both of us to take a nap." "Why?"

So why write this book? Why write any book? Why do anything in life? The "why" question is the crucially important question of motive, of desire. Ultimately it's about our heart—the soul of our leadership, including our communication.

I have learned from many people that the one main answer to any "why" question is to love and serve others—to buy and prepare food for them, to share a meal with them, to provide space for them to rest, and even to write a book that might help them be better, more fulfilled, and more grateful leaders. In my experience, all of the great questions ultimately come down to caring for and about others—what in the book I call excellence and compassion. These are not just chores; they are callings that require us to open our hearts and minds to the service of others. This is where grace enters the picture of life. Even a three-year-old grandson can carry grace simply by being what such a boy is supposed to be—a joy, a delight, and an interrogator.

I just returned home from walking in a rain shower that caught me off guard. Grace is like that. It is coming down all around us and on us, often very unexpectedly. My debts of gratitude are in the many drops, some from storms, others from gentle showers. Only when the rain has temporarily stopped and I have finished writing do I have time to reflect on the grace in it all. Grace is like that too. There are enough drops of grace to fill this book, let alone the acknowledgements. Blessings to all who have served me beyond the dry confines of my evaporating memory—even if, like three-year-old Elliot, you don't yet know how your raindrops served me.

Contents

Foreword

Quentin Schultze has crafted a remarkable book that the great poet W. H. Auden (1907–73) would have loved. It combines heart, intellect, and story—all carefully crafted with inspiring language in short chapters that you can read quickly and then savor and learn from again and again. Even if you've never read Auden, you need to read and ponder Schultze's wonderful little book. It will become a classic on communication for real leaders and followers alike. Robert Greenleaf, the founder of servant leadership would have loved it as well—as I'll discuss shortly.

What do Schultze and Auden have in common? First, in Auden's writings, the urbane, the common, the parochial, the cosmic, the everyday, the erudite, the personal, the public, the inner, the outer mingle with great fluency. Similarly, in Schultze's book the scholarly urbane and grandma's grassroots wisdom slot into one another in a magical and memorable way. Schultze uses stories from his own life of failure and success as folk-like parables brimming with wisdom.

Second, although Schultze's writing does not display the metaphorical opulence of Auden (Who could compete with such a gifted poet?), both are masters of metaphor. Two of the greatest scientists in history, Isaac Newton and Charles Darwin, won over the world not by sheer science but by the metaphors they used to communicate their findings in the two most influential books in the history of science—Newton's *Principia* (1687) and Darwin's *On the Origin of Species* (1859). Newton told the apple anecdote four times in his lifetime—of sitting in an orchard and having an apple fall on his head. He didn't publish his theory of gravity until twenty years after he said the apple incident happened, but it was the apple metaphor that sold the theory. Likewise, Charles Darwin worked twenty years on a single book after spending five years aboard a ship named the *Beagle*. He didn't communicate his evolutionary theories in scientific papers but in literary forms that were not just freighted with metaphor but formed by it. Schultze uses metaphors carefully, meaningfully, in each chapter; apples fall on his and the reader's heads.

Third, Auden had an eye for the particular, for the memento or the moment that could serve as a passport to the universal. For both Auden and Schultze, objects are not mere objects; things swim within the stream of life and, like living beings, have an emotional charge or tone for us. Schultze has a gift for communicating extraordinary insights about ordinary life.

Fourth, for both Auden and Schultze there is no looking away from the human capacity for cruelty and evil. In "Letters from Iceland" (1937), Auden evoked a scene in which he observed the slaughter of an enormous, gentle whale, "the most beautiful animal I have ever seen." While the whale was being cut up on the slipway, Auden heard a bell clang, and immediately, "everyone stuck their spades in the carcass and went off to lunch. The body remained alone in the sun, the flesh still steaming a little." Auden reflected that the scene evoked "an extraordinary vision of the cold controlled ferocity of the human species." For Schultze, leadership is not forged in the crucible of the fashionably hot, but in the smithy of the Spirit that hammers the letter "e" onto the end of the word "human." Only a humane leader can truly serve. Only a compassionate listener can love.

Fifth, Schultze and Auden have listened to and learned from some of the most trenchant theologians on the planet. Auden was greatly influenced by his friend Reinhold Niebuhr. Schultze doesn't cloud this book with footnotes, but it's obvious that he reads, ponders, and breathes theological insight. I've spent my adult life reading theology and rarely have I seen so much theological understanding expressed so winsomely in such a compact book. Each brief chapter is like a daily meditation on grace, truth, and the human condition. For me, reading this book was a spiritual experience. That's a testament to the depth of Schultze's understanding of leadership as stewardship, and communication as communion.

I was one of the last people to visit Robert Greenleaf (1904–90), to whom this book is dedicated and whose spirit shines through on every page Schultze writes. The day I sought his counsel about the future of higher education, he wouldn't let me leave until I had helped him clean his shelves of some boxes of his books he wanted to give away before he died. He graciously made it seem as if I was doing him a favor rather than receiving the honor of having part of his collection now as part of mine. Greenleaf is buried in Terre Haute, Indiana, with an epitaph that captures the spirit of this book—its humor, its ad hominem wisdom, its humanity, its humbleness:

Potentially a good plumber;
ruined by a sophisticated education.

Leonard Sweet
Drew University, George Fox University, Tabor College

Introduction

I wrote this book for everyone who wants to become a better communicator and a successful leader.

I suggest that you read one of the 30 short "meditations" each day and respond personally to my questions at the end of each one. Jot down on the page just one way you will improve your communication. By writing it down, you are much more likely to do it. Trust me.

Over time, your marked-up copy of the book will become your own, personalized guide to great communication. After you complete your guide, take a few minutes to browse your notes once a month to refresh your memory and keep yourself on track. Add notes about your successes in real life. You will discover that you are becoming the kind of communicator you always wanted to be.

Others will notice your superior communication. They will want to become like you. And to follow you.

In this book I tell many personal stories. I open my heart and soul. I share failures as well as successes.

I have lived a rich professional life. I have been an author, college professor, speaker, media producer, publisher, media critic, business owner, and consultant. I've learned a tremendous amount by mentoring people in communication-related professions. Mentoring, like teaching, is one of the best ways to learn.

But I grew up in a very dysfunctional family with an alcoholic father and a schizophrenic mother. I had much to overcome. Even up to college I was introverted and socially awkward. So I studied engineering partly to hide out with introverts.

Eventually I took some courses on communication that changed my life and vocation. I discovered that studying communication could help me personally as well as professionally. But I needed to be honest, open, and courageous. I had to venture outside of myself and into challenging relationships. I doubted myself, but I felt increasingly liberated. I hope that by reading this book you will too.

I learned that others often see in us the very capacities that we don't see in ourselves. I discovered that personal weaknesses could become marvelous strengths. My difficult family background deepened my empathy for colleagues, students, and mentees.

Teaching became partly a way of serving students who, like me in my college days, lacked self-confidence, were afraid of taking personal and professional risks, and suffered from social awkwardness.

Along the way, I started mentoring and consulting for leaders. I served everyone from Internet CEOs to newly minted preachers, and from academic administrators to government and media leaders. I also launched successful businesses and served on boards. Each of these activities was another opportunity for me to use my developing communication skills to serve others.

I became what I call a "servant communicator." I hope

you will hear the same high calling and come to know the rewards of heeding it. If you develop your communication skills and use them to serve others, you will have a gratifying life.

I didn't seek to become a mentor. Others saw me as a mentor, and I became one. I practiced empathetic listening. I realized that by seeking to be a respectable and available person, I had become someone whom others trusted and sought out for guidance. And as they trusted me, I became more trusting.

I now see leadership primarily as healthy, responsible communication in one's current life—not as a lofty position only for unusually gifted or privileged persons. To lead is to accept responsibility and act responsibly. You can become such a worthy leader.

Surveys galore document that communication skills are critically important for professional success in nearly all fields. Communication is the most important leadership skill. Unfortunately, great communication does not come naturally for most people. It takes the kind of soul-searching honesty discussed in this book.

My understanding of leadership soared when I first read Robert K. Greenleaf's *Servant Leadership: A Journey into the Nature of Legitimate Power and Greatness* (Greenleaf preferred the title "The Leader as Servant"). Every page offered insight about leadership *and* communication. Here was someone who, like me, believed that leadership was less a particular career track than an approach to life, and less a matter of purely technical know-how than of wisdom.

Greenleaf's work captivated my heart, touched my soul, and fed my mind. I wanted to return the favor by passing along the wisdom. This book is one way I have done so.

I decided to begin each entry in this book with a relevant quote from Greenleaf's fertile writings. The book is made up of 30 days of my jazz-like improvisations based on Greenleaf's themes.

I believe that all who gratefully accept the gift of communication and seek to use it conscientiously to serve others well are de facto leaders, regardless of where they serve and their official title. Like me, they might be what former Herman Miller CEO Max DePree calls "roving leaders" who lead here and there as circumstances permit, and frequently by example (*The Art of Leadership*).

I wrote this book to speak to your heart, not just your mind. All of our communication begins in our hearts. Please open yours as you read each day's entry. Be honest with yourself. And hopeful. Your past doesn't dictate your future—no more than mine did.

Thank you for joining me on the journey. I hope to continue to serve you well with my future writing and speaking. Please visit my website-blog (www.quentinschultze.com) to sign up for updates, including valuable material beyond the content of this book.

This book can also serve discussion groups. Please consider forming one.

In order to protect personal identities I have changed key elements in many of the stories in this book.

I hope *Communicate Like a True Leader* will help you become an increasingly grateful, skilled, servant-oriented communicator. May your own journey become a wonderful legacy of satisfying service.

Citation Abbreviations

(OB) Greenleaf, Robert K. *On Becoming a Servant Leader.*
Edited by Don M. Frick and Larry C. Spears. San Francisco:
Jossey-Bass, 1996.

(PS) Greenleaf, Robert K. *The Power of Servant Leadership.*
Edited by Larry C. Spears. San Francisco: Berrett-Koehler,
1998.

(RG) Frick, Don M. *Robert K. Greenleaf: A Life of Servant
Leadership.* San Francisco: Berrett-Koehler, 2004.

(SL) Greenleaf, Robert K. *Servant Leadership: A Journey into the
Nature of Legitimate Power and Greatness.* New York: Paulist
Press, 1977.

(SS) Greenleaf, Robert K. *Seeker and Servant: Reflections on
Religious Leadership.* Edited by Anne T. Fraker and Larry C.
Spears. San Francisco: Jossey-Bass, 1996.

1

Celebrating the Gift

"Hold in your mind the attitude of awe and wonder before the great ineffable mystery of creation of which we are all a part." (RG, p. 237)

Some years ago I met with former Herman Miller CEO Max DePree to discuss communication. I humbly wanted to confer about his splendid definition of leadership in *The Art of Leadership*: "The first responsibility of a leader is to define reality. The last is to say thank you. In between the two, the leader must become a servant and a debtor."

I had concluded personally that DePree's definition should begin with the right attitude: gratitude. Real leaders are grateful ones. They are a joy to follow. And they are more effective.

So I asked DePree if he thought that maybe the attitude of gratitude should come before "defining reality" in his definition of leadership. I suggested that the amended definition of leadership begin something like this: "The first responsibility of a leader is to accept gratefully the call to serve others."

He quickly agreed. I was relieved. And grateful.

Why is such preliminary thankfulness important? Why not include gratitude just in the last part of DePree's definition?

Because gratitude gets to the basic demeanor of a servant-minded communicator. Being grateful is a heartfelt way of living and growing. It's the soil from which the best communication grows.

What should a leader give thanks for? Certainly for the opportunity to serve others. For a place and time and people to lead.

A leader should also be thankful for the gift of communication itself. We couldn't lead or follow without it.

We can give thanks for the many people who contributed to our own abilities to communicate. Consider the roles of grandparents and parents, siblings, teachers, colleagues, neighbors, book authors, and so on. To borrow from DePree, our debts are deep.

Finally, consider what the gift of communication has meant for our relationships. Because we can communicate (same root word as "commune") with one another, we are not relegated to loneliness. We can play and work with others. We can share jokes and joys, trials and tragedies, hopes and dreams. We can encourage and forgive, plan and practice everything from weddings to strategy meetings. We can define leadership with others and then seek together to live out our definition in service of others. And we can revise the definition as we go along.

Communication is a spectacular gift that we inherit from generation to generation and from organization to organization—even from conversation to conversation.

To be the kind of leader whose heart is bathed in gratitude is to accept the most fitting beginning for a daily life of service—giving thanks. We know this deep in our hearts. This is why we all seek, even unconsciously, to be around thankful persons. We sense they are grateful for good things, including us. We want to be like them.

So a servant leader communicates with a sense of what Robert K. Greenleaf calls "awe and wonder." Her communication begins and ends with heart-opening gratitude. Gratitude is the missing first chapter in books about communication.

Reflection

Does your communication reflect a grateful heart? Write down the names of two persons who passed along to you the gift of communication. Keep adding to the list as you review your notes in this book. Let your gratitude grow.

2

Accepting the Call to Care

"Having power (and every trustee has some power) one
initiates the means whereby power is used to serve and not to
hurt . . . in the sense that all who are touched . . . become . . .
healthier, wiser, freer, more autonomous, more likely
themselves to become servants." (SL, p. 130)

I got my first regular job at 16 years of age, assisting a 45-
ish man who ran a family-owned pharmacy in Chicago.
Jerry was the pharmacist and manager. He was also a friend
to locals who came in to buy newspapers, talk politics, and
share jokes.

In addition to cleaning and restocking shelves, I washed
pharmaceutical pill bottles and removed the manufacturers'
labels so Jerry could reuse them to fill prescriptions. I spent
Saturday mornings soaking bottles and scraping off labels.

After months of Saturdays I asked Jerry why he didn't
just buy new bottles. He suggested that my work served him,
the business, customers, and society. Why load up landfills

with more glass (there was no recycling)? He added that all human work impacts others.

The importance of what we did, Jerry explained, included the greater meaning of the work, not merely the skill involved, however seemingly menial. He said that much of his pharmacy work was pretty routine. In the bigger picture, though, he was actually keeping people healthy, and I was helping him help them.

I believe that we humans are called to be stewards or, as Robert K. Greenleaf put it, trustees. We are all called to be caretakers of the world we've inherited. We don't ultimately "own" the world even though we do acquire parts of it to use and enjoy. To put it differently, we're all entrepreneurs who serve others by creating additional worth out of the value that was here long before we were even born.

Moreover, we conduct our caretaking in and through communication. Jerry's store depended on in-person, written, and telephone communication to serve customers, staff, and the broader community.

Caretaking has two aspects. The first is caring *for* others. This caring is excellence in action. We become skilled at whatever specifically we're called to do, including communication. We listen well, speak carefully, write clearly, and persuade effectively as needed to serve others.

The second aspect of caretaking is caring *about* others— engaging our heart in our work, with compassion. A true professional needs to care about those she is serving.

Jerry was not just called to be a pharmacist. He cared for and about his customers and employees.

Every leader as caretaker-trustee must be a skilled and caring communicator. These two aspects of caretaking—

excellence and *compassion*—are twin anchors for servant leadership. We learn through communication what they are and how to practice them.

At the time I was too new to the world of work to recognize how fortunate I was to learn caretaking from a true leader like Jerry. Twenty years after he closed the Chicago store and moved to California, I visited him there to thank him personally for caring for and about me. Thanks to Jerry, I became wiser, freer, healthier, and a more autonomous communicator.

Reflection

Do you have a deep sense of your calling as a caretaker? Do you need more skill (excellence) or heart (compassion)—or both?

3

Listening to Reality

"Simply practice being aware. Look, and be still. Feel, and be still. Listen, and be still." (OB, p. 36)

I was a mediocre college freshman. I went to class, studied for exams, and submitted assignments on time. But my grades still suffered. I was baffled.

During the beginning of my sophomore year, I started reviewing each day's class notes after classes were over. I soon realized how little I recalled even of that day's lectures and discussions. It dawned on me that normal note-taking merely gave me the impression that I was learning.

I implemented a strategy that revolutionized my learning, launched me successfully into graduate school, helped me become a solid teacher, equipped me to be a productive researcher-writer, and made it possible for me to be an engaging speaker.

I not only reviewed my notes daily. I rewrote them from

scratch within a couple of hours of each class meeting. I used my actual course notes as prompts to recall more of the lecture and to help me organize my own reactions to the material. My notes expanded. My retention swelled.

My revised notes became a kind of journal of my dialogue with the instructor and the readings. I integrated into my revised course notes my daily reading notes, reworking them into language that was meaningful to me, and preparing to ask the instructor at the next class anything that I was uncertain about. From then on I earned nearly straight A's with far less cramming for exams.

Moreover, I had begun journaling about my learning—one of the most important communication skills. I became a real learner by discovering how to pay attention to others and myself.

In a broad sense, I learned how to listen. Listening is *attending to reality*. It's the best antidote to superficial communication. All research and marketing are based on the idea of attending to reality.

Also, we need to attend to both our outer and inner realities. We need to listen to others. But we also need to listen to what our own hearts and minds are telling us—listening to ourselves.

True, honest listening, either to the world outside or to the world inside of us, opens us up to seeing reality as it is rather than as we want to see it.

My revolutionized note-taking system, essentially a form of journaling, became a way of listening to others and myself at the same time. I still take such notes about my everyday communication.

The goal in listening, deeply understood, is to get to

know reality less promiscuously and more intimately. A wise person gains an understanding of reality before acting. A fool plows ahead without first attending to reality. During my freshman year I was a foolish student, going through academic motions without actually listening to others or myself.

Only when we get to know others well are we able to know how to serve others as particular persons.

Only when we know ourselves well do we know how we, as individuals, can personally serve them with excellence and compassion.

We can't really serve in the abstract. It makes no sense for me to say I serve the concept of my wife; I need to be able to serve her as a special individual, the ways that she individually is best served. All knowing—all listening to reality—is predicated on this idea of becoming intimate with the subject, whether a person, a body of knowledge, or a specific skill.

Excessive chatter squelches intimate knowing. Those who like to hear themselves tend not to hear others. Those who like to listen only to others lose track of who they are.

The monastics had it right: speak only if you can improve upon the silence.

Otherwise we shall be fools.

Reflection

How would you honestly assess your own ability to attend to reality by listening? How much time do you actually spend daily reflecting on what you are learning about yourself and about other persons and organizations?

4

Seeking Shared Understanding

"Nothing is meaningful to me until it is related to my own experience." (OB, p. 304)

As a new professor in Grand Rapids, Michigan, I was sitting in my campus office when the administrative assistant asked if I could take a call from a radio station in Zeeland.

Seconds later a program producer with an interesting accent invited me to a radio interview the following day. I accepted.

The next day the host came on the line to introduce me to his audience. I couldn't fully understand him. His accent plus the static reduced intelligibility. He frustratingly asked me, "Do you know anything about . . . Zealand?"

"Of course," I responded, "it's just down the road. I've spoken in Zeeland a couple of times." "Huh?" he wondered aloud. "Aren't you in Michigan, in the USA?" "Right," I confirmed. "Grand Rapids. About 20 miles from Zeeland."

I had assumed that the program was broadcast on a nearby station in Zeeland, Michigan, when in fact it was a national broadcast on Radio New Zealand. What I interpreted as a Dutch accent from my own geographic area was a Kiwi dialect.

Miscommunication knows few bounds. The basic problem is that we assume that there will be shared understanding even when we all bring different assumptions and life experiences to our interactions.

The most essential part of any definition of communication is *shared understanding*. Human communication is first of all the art of establishing shared understanding. To understand someone is to "stand under" that unique person, to humble one's self to his understanding of reality.

Communication is not merely the "effect" that we have on one other. How you interpret me—how you are "affected" by my words—is not necessarily communication. If you don't understand what I am actually intending to say, we failed to communicate. Such lack of shared understanding is *miscommunication*, not communication.

This is critically important because we humans are not called merely to affect one another. We are creatures of meaning, trust, and, at our best, shared understanding. Which is to say we are designed for community.

We don't have to agree with one another in order to understand one another. Mature persons can agree to disagree even when they deeply understand each other.

Shared understanding can begin when we honestly accept one another's invitations to engagement. We are on the way when we accept such invitations gratefully, listen openly, and converse respectfully. We thereby foster shared understanding—understanding of each other's intended meanings.

When I began the radio interview I didn't know who my audience really was. New Zealand was beyond my frame of reference. As I wrapped up the interview, I was sweating profusely. I had no idea how well the audience understood me. I could barely remember the conversation. I had been swimming anxiously in a sea of miscommunication. Ironically, the interview was about communication.

Reflection

Do you see communication as shared understanding or mere impact? Do you routinely aim for shared understanding in your everyday interactions?

5

Giving Up Control

"We are acting on the principle that knowledge, not the spirit, is power. Knowledge is but a tool. The spirit is the essence."
(PS, p. 25)

I receive humbling notes from former mentees thanking me for something I said to them. Sometimes I don't recall saying exactly such things. They sound like something I might have said, but not precisely what I think I would have shared.

When we listen we often emphasize particular points in our own minds. We tend to note and elaborate on those thoughts that seem to best address our own situations. In this sense, human communication is somewhat idiosyncratic. Thirty people who attend the same meeting will pick up on points that are most important to each of them.

While this can lead to misunderstanding, it can also enhance our communication. Others can use our words to expand and improve upon what we have to say.

Recognizing this dynamic, I assume that others might be ready to receive more than what I strictly intend to say. In fact, what I have to say might stimulate in listeners significantly more understanding than what I think I have to offer.

In short, human communication is *dialogue*, not merely *monologue*. Even if the listener doesn't say anything, I can assume that he is probably in dialogue with himself—thinking, reflecting, questioning and the like. He might even be getting more out of his own inner dialogue than I thought I was capable of sharing.

Robert Greenleaf refers to the role of "spirit" in relationships. I believe that when we aim humbly to serve others through communication, we discover an expansive, creative reality that can enhance our communication. In this sense, to lead from within us is also to be led from outside of or beyond us. Where this communication-enhancing creativity comes from is a mystery. So "spirit" seems to be an appropriate term.

With such creativity comes a great irony: sometimes the more stringently we try to control our communication, the less communication we will experience. This is counterintuitive. We need to reserve space for the unexpected—both in our speaking and our listening.

Of course such unpredictable communication isn't an excuse for sloppiness. As I suggested earlier, we are called to use the gift of communication to serve others excellently as well as compassionately. Yet if we work too hard at it we might miss out on the unexpected benefits, even beyond our apparent abilities. We have to give up some control to be open to greater creative possibilities. Controlling people are not the most effective—let alone the most joyful—communicators. They tend to squelch the creative spirit.

Reflection

Can you recall a time when communication transcended your expectations—when people received more from your intended message than what you imagined was possible? If not, are you truly open to communication beyond your own means of control?

6

Persuading Respectfully

"Both leader and follower respect the autonomy and integrity
of the other and each allows and encourages the other to find
his or her own intuitive confirmation of the rightness of the
belief or action." (PS, p. 85)

I have read extensively the writings of Saint Augustine of
Hippo (354–430). His books, letters, and sermons are
among the most influential in the Western world.

Before becoming a Christian, priest, and eventually
bishop, Augustine was a public rhetorician and teacher. He
employed ancient Greek and Roman rhetorical skills to serve
lawyers and politicians.

Augustine didn't care if his clients' messages were true.
In fact, he felt that successfully persuading someone to believe a false statement was a worthy, career-building goal. For
instance, if he persuaded a judge to believe that a guilty man
was innocent, Augustine thought he himself was a terrific

communicator. He was thereby a real professional.

After his spiritual turnaround, however, Augustine felt grave misgivings about his work. He wondered if persuasion was ever moral. Today this might be like a legendary advertising copywriter joining a synagogue, sitting under a wise rabbi, and feeling convicted that it was time to give up advertising.

Augustine's era was similar to ours. Most people accepted the necessity of persuasion. Many were willing to take advantage of their audiences.

Augustine eventually concluded that persuasion is not inherently evil. The question for him became how to practice it rightly, not just effectively.

For me, this is critically important. Servant leaders should practice communication by loving their audiences as their *neighbors*—by treating others as they desire to be treated.

The Hasidic philosopher Martin Buber said in *I and Thou* that we tend to imagine our communication partner either as a mere thing (as an "It") or as a truly human person of inherent value (as a "Thou").

When we employ our voices, pens, or keypads, we treat others as particular kinds of creatures. If we conceive of them as fully human, like us, we will approach them very differently than if we see them as beneath our own dignity.

Today some public figures use mass and social media derogatorily to attack opponents. They employ nasty, self-serving language. Like Augustine's clients, they retain professional communication consultants to twist and turn evocative symbols.

We dwell, like Augustine, in a swamp of foul communication. The situation can appear hopeless. Many college students, not even fully corrupted by the market of malice, commonly stretch the truth on their résumés. So do some CEOs.

A servant leader persuades with the best interests of others in mind. She avoids purely self-serving messaging. She respects audiences by loving them as neighbors. She thereby treats others as she wishes to be treated.

Reflection

Which persons do you treat with the most respect (each is a "Thou" in your life)? With the least respect (each is an "It")? When you answer the latter question, consider whether or not you are being truly honest with yourself; self-deception lurks everywhere.

7

Painting a Vision

"Visions, both good and bad, can be contagious." (PS, p. 43)

In the mid-1990s the board of a media organization asked me to speak with directors and management about the future of digital media.

I prepared a presentation for them—about the history of media.

I explained that new media forms rarely replace earlier ones. Instead, new technologies alter how people use previous ones while adopting new ones. In short, a vision for the future should include the changing roles of both older and newer media.

The board asked excellent questions, discussed growth opportunities in the expanding media landscape, and asked me to serve as a consultant to help paint a vision for the organization's future. Soon the organization was successfully transitioning to the emerging media world. This happened because of the leadership's realistic and contagious vision.

A solid vision is a painting of the future. It calls people together for a shared mission.

Establishing an organization's vision is an essential act of leadership communication. It's an art, not a science. It's more qualitative than quantitative. A vision is not a precise goal, but an image of a shared and noble future. It's an evocative metaphor, like an architect's watercolor rendering of a potential new headquarters building.

As a college teacher, each semester I painted a vision of myself and my students as members of a hospitable community of mutual service and shared learning. When I taught public speaking, I said that we were called together to learn how to serve audiences, not merely to learn how to speak well.

One of my professor friends who uses a motorized wheelchair for mobility wonderfully cultivates a vision of service in the classroom. He visualizes the shared neediness of the entire class—the dependence of each student on every other student for the sake of mutual learning. His visible disability provides the authentic vision for all students to use as they explore how to be more whole by leveraging their differences in a shared enterprise.

When my wife graduated from seminary, I presented her with a John Swanson serigraph of Psalm 23—"Though I walk through the valley of the shadow of death." It was a fitting vision for her as she progressed toward becoming a hospice chaplain. Swanson describes the scene as follows: "Moving forward barefoot and without fear, the two figures travel through a valley transformed by their own beliefs; a world where lions and lambs can lay together in peaceful harmony.

This story connects with our own lives. . . . For even though we walk through the valley of the shadow of death, we fear no evil, for God is with us."

In this vision as I imagined it, the patient and chaplain are traveling partners, expectantly traversing a valley. They walk steadfastly on the common spiritual trail that will eventually take them both to the Promised Land. Like chaplains and hospice patients, we all live not just by bread alone, but also by visions of what is possible.

Ducks Unlimited's vision is "wetlands sufficient to fill the skies with waterfowl today, tomorrow and forever." The words paint a palpable image of nature's flourishing. It's a hospitable, seductive vision that fosters a community of people mutually dedicated to a wetland-rich, waterfowl-full future.

Reflection

Do you have sufficient words to paint a contagious vision for yourself—who you are and whom you serve? If so, write it down and memorize it. If not, work on one, starting with just one key word that describes your vision for yourself.

8

Meditating Reflectively

"For a big idea to evolve, I have found that a big chunk of
meditative time is required." (PS, p. 274–75)

Primarily because of an abusive childhood, I spent years in
therapy. But I never really experienced life-changing
inner transformation until I also began journaling about my
life. Each morning I would read spiritual material, give
thanks, browse recent journal entries, add a journal entry if it
seemed fitting, and then mindfully review my schedule for the
day.

I realized over time that by journaling candidly about
myself (listening to my inner reality) I was coming to know
myself much better. I could identify my strengths and weaknesses by reviewing my own actions and other people's re-
sponses. Journal entries became focused mirrors. My thera-
pist's observations, which I also jotted in my journal, became
another voice in my daily meditations.

I discovered that this type of meditation gave me the space to nurture empathy toward others, especially those I had hurt or could hurt. In a sense, my wounds helped me to learn how to serve other wounded hearts. I became an admittedly wounded leader.

My meditative practices make me a more humble follower and a more worthy leader. Most noticeably, I am slower to speak from my ego during the day and much faster to listen to and appreciate others' contributions.

I believe that a leader will serve others more deeply and honestly when he learns how to meditate on the good and the bad.

For me, solitude is essential. I need focus, without interruptions. I can't even listen to music and mediate at the same time. "To do anything reflectively," writes Robert Greenleaf, "demands that one be alone with one's thoughts and accept the presence of a deeper self with which one may have only tenuous communication" (OB, 43).

The times I have been most professionally productive were two sabbatical years. In those years I charted a vocationally countercultural course, framing my work within my meditative life, without feeling rushed.

Over time, regular note taking became an essential part of my life. I wrote brief notes during the day about my everyday victories and defeats. I then included some of those notes in my morning journaling, prefacing them with my initial and a colon: "Q:." That means essentially, "Note to self: listen up."

My children gave me a shirt-pocket "briefcase" that holds a few index cards and provides enough backing for writing on the cards. This older technology, which I carry everywhere, provides a quick and easy way to make notes for review. But it also reminds me by its presence to reflect on the quality of my everyday communication. The briefcase-pad is both a technology and a symbol.

With the note cards, daily reflection, and journaling, I have a system for keeping me personally honest and growing as a servant-oriented communicator. If I don't regularly and courageously communicate with myself, I lose track of who I am and what I am called to do as a humble steward.

Meditation engages my mind and also opens my heart. I become a less self-centered and a more compassionate servant. It expands my sense of reality to include the grace that I can't manufacture, only identify and accept.

"The asking of the right question, reflectively," Greenleaf says of meditation, "is the conscious means whereby a new internal climate is created, a climate in which a new constructive attitude might be born and grow" (OB, 43).

Reflection

How well you are doing personally on your journey toward becoming a true communicator? Write out your thoughts. Honestly.

9

Conversing Well

"Approach the relationship with the attitude of acceptance
that oneself, the persuader, may change." (OB, pp. 143–44)

The thing that struck me the most about the first board of
directors I served on was the amount of conversation.
Conversation. Not hard-nosed business analysis. Not reviewing minutes and spreadsheets. Not even covering items
on an approved agenda. Open conversation about company-
related matters.

Initially I thought that such conversation was frivolous.
But soon I learned that conversation was essential. Among
other things, conversation fostered mutually respectful relationships, created a nonthreatening climate, nurtured democratic deliberation and decision-making, contributed to shared
understanding, and added considerable delight to the pro-
ceedings.

I discovered that even the most challenging issues and

potential matters of disagreement were best addressed in the context of open conversation. Informal discussion is a timely resource.

Leaders must master conversation. There is no substitute. A leader who can't carry on a warm, engaging conversation is a liability.

Conversing well is like playing jazz music—variations on engaging themes. A leader begins the composition and, if needed, swings individuals' improvisations back to the major themes. Along the way, the servant leader enjoys the music. She refrains from seeking control and is open to being influenced. She practices dialogue, not monologue.

For newcomers to an organization, conversation is the least intimidating path to participation. For project managers and group leaders, a conversational culture offers meaningful, autonomous, practical participation in the mission and purpose of the organization. For executives and trustees, conversation is the most conducive context for mutual listening and decision-making.

Open, respectful conversation says to all participants that their thoughts matter. It helps us to climb out of our loneliness, fear, and egocentrism to form community.

Perhaps the rise of coffee shops during the computer age reflects the unquenchable human desire for conversation. Coffee is a symbol for warm, open conversation. Sitting alone at a computer all day, firing off and receiving waves of emails and text messages, reviewing complicated spreadsheets, and filling in online and intradocument forms all seem to create a demand for conversational breaks. In today's high-tech culture we need food and drink to nourish our conversational lives as well as our bodies.

Text messaging is not a worthy substitute for in-person conversation. Excessive texting might even stunt our growth as conversationalists.

Good conversation does not happen automatically. We have to learn how to avoid such misstarts as gossiping, judging, and venting. We also must teach ourselves to hold back and to listen for understanding before expressing ourselves. Ego and interruptions kill conversation. So does asking questions designed to elicit particular, obvious answers. Pedantic language squelches the democratic spirit of conversation.

Reflection

When was the last time you had a terrific conversation with someone at work? What factors helped you to participate well—such as openness, honesty, respect, and freedom?

10

Risking Face

"I submit that *all* masks chafe; I never saw a well-fitting mask.
It is a great relief to take them off." (PS, p. 74)

A fine friend and skilled speaker landed in a dreadful situation. He had agreed to address a convention of toastmasters—persons who lead local public-speaking clubs where members overcome common speaking fears and practice effective speaking techniques.

When he arrived a few minutes early for the event, he met with his friend who had arranged the speech. He discovered that the audience was not toastmasters, but postmasters—persons who run local post offices.

He frantically tried to organize a speech in his head while his friend introduced him. Then he took the stage, mic in hand, alone with the whole audience of postmasters peering directly at him. What could he possibly do?

He relinquished his façade. He explained that he had

planned a speech for the wrong audience. That he didn't even know what postmasters actually do. That he was thoroughly unprepared.

Then he spoke from the heart about what he knew intimately. He told stories about his and his close friends' loneliness. About their fears. About the stifling lack of meaning in their work.

My friend's message was simple but profound: we are all first and foremost human beings, not workers. We share a common humanity. We experience fear as well as hope.

Then he thanked the postmasters for the opportunity to share his thoughts and feelings. He received a long, standing ovation. The wounded storyteller had connected with the wounded postmasters.

When we put on masks we deprive others and ourselves of the shared benefits of genuine community.

But opening up is not easy. We are fearful of what others will think about us. It's easier to posture and pretend.

Of course we can be too candid. Like some airline passengers, leaders can spend far too much time talking about themselves. Learning appropriate self-disclosure is essential. We need to reveal enough personally to connect with others in our shared humanity, but not so much that our conversations and presentations become self-performed soap operas.

For most of us, however, the problem is excessive fear of rejection. Once we begin taking off our masks, we expose our inner selves to others' inspection. The risks seem daunting.

Admitting that our masks make us frauds is essential for all leaders who seek to communicate authentically. Only then can we begin to construct genuine selves that are worthy of what others might think about us in our best moments. The result is not another façade. It's a genuine person who can laugh at being miss-prepared for a speech and yet connect with the audience as fellow humans.

Once I was in the audience when my friend who had spoken to the postmasters was speaking to another group. After his presentation he came up to me unexpectedly with a signed copy of his latest book. I was deeply honored. I quickly looked at the signature page of the book while he was smiling at me and noticed that he had misspelled my name. What should I do?

I couldn't ask him for a new copy, properly endorsed. I could affirm our shared humanity. "Bill," I said, "thanks so much. The fact that you misspelled my name is about the highest honor I could receive from you. Neither of us needs to save face, because of your open heart. I love you." We laughed. And hugged. And laughed some more.

Reflection

Why are you fearful of being open with others? What are you covering up?

11

Forming Integrity

"The person who says, 'Now I am being ethical,' should be regarded with suspicion." (OB, p. 167)

The head of an advertising agency asked me to conduct focus groups about the impact of a bank's statewide advertising campaign. He said he wanted to evaluate the effectiveness of the expensive campaign on consumers' perceptions of the bank.

When we met, he produced an ironclad confidentiality agreement for me to sign. The gist of it was that I would be prevented from talking with anyone about the research.

The good news for me as a communication scholar was that the advertising campaign had already been a major effort. I figured that just about everyone in the state was familiar with the campaign. I jumped at the chance to explore the impact of the omnipresent commercials.

A legendary slice of wisdom in communication research

holds that all publicity is good publicity. Publicity generates interest. It sells books and movie tickets—and much more.

The focus groups revealed that nearly everyone hated the advertisements. They detested the jingle. They strongly felt that the commercials made fun of state residents as country bumpkins. I never had heard such thoroughly negative appraisals of a public campaign. The advertisements produced tremendous name recognition for the bank while simultaneously tarnishing the company's image. I wondered if all publicity truly is good publicity.

I called the agency months later to see if my research had helped the creative people "fine-tune" the campaign. The CEO told me that all was well with the current campaign. The client was pleased.

Soon thereafter, I happened to meet one of the bank officials at a social gathering. Of course I couldn't say anything about my research. A promise is a promise. I talked about other things.

The heart of integrity is being true to ourselves so we can be true to others. Persons with integrity have a strong inner sense of who they are and live in tune with themselves. Their actions radiate from the genuineness of their being.

In my view, the agency leaders seemed to lack integrity. They professed that they wanted to know the truth about their major advertising campaign, but then they apparently failed to act upon that truth with their client when they didn't receive the results they wanted from me.

A leader who lacks integrity is a communicative chameleon, saying what others want to hear and what is immediately expedient. Such a person lives at the mercy of the latest crises: "What have I said recently to different people?"

"How can I keep others from knowing about this problem?"

Trying to become all things to all people, the disintegrated leader eventually becomes nothing to anyone in particular. Such a misguided leader becomes a director of duplicities.

But lack of integrity is not just other people's problem. All of us fall short. We are not whole.

The good news is, every one of us can grow toward wholeness through many small but wise decisions. Integrity is all about putting our lives back together each day. Keeping company with upright persons helps. Then, when we speak and act with integrity, others will know where we stand. And so will we. We will rightly say what we mean, and mean what we say—and live what we profess.

Integrity produces personal peace. I couldn't fix the advertising campaign, let alone the advertising agency, but I could live in peace knowing that I was true to the client and myself. I did good work and kept my promise. There was no reason to regard me with suspicion.

Reflection

How would you assess the gap between what you profess and how you act? How would your colleagues?

12

Being Natural

"The most important lesson I have learned about maturity is
that the emergence, the full development, of what is uniquely
me should be an important concern throughout my entire
life." (PS, p. 62)

One of the most inspiring aspects of my own journey has
been serving rising leaders, including seminary graduates. Most seminarians become parish pastors and quickly
serve as leaders by virtue of how their congregations view the
office of pastor. There are few professions where leadership
is similarly thrust upon relatively unprepared persons so
quickly. The failure rate is high.

I have helped seminary graduates with one of the most
formidable tasks they face as leaders: preaching. The most
important thing I learned about coaching them is helping
them be themselves. They tend to adopt a forced style in tune
with their sense of higher calling. They forget that they are

particular, human vessels—individual persons.

A similar malady can afflict any rising leader. In my experience, the slicker and more stereotypical the speaker, the shallower the communication. The more natural and humbly self-assured the speaker, the deeper the communication.

So I advise speakers to develop their own style in tune with who they actually are rather than whom they want to be like. Naturalness trumps affectedness.

The same holds for our everyday interactions. Style matters considerably. Affected styles make others uncomfortable. When we try to impress, we generally disappoint. We fail to live up to our own stylistic hype. This is not primarily an issue of content or message per se. It's a more slippery matter of how we conduct ourselves.

As far as I know, the only way to address this effectively is to hone and strengthen our natural speaking and interacting style. We accept who we are and work on becoming more naturally articulate, lucid, and expressive.

The beauty of this approach to becoming a better communicator is that we can begin immediately working on how well we are communicating. We don't have to imitate or impress people. We can instead consider if our demeanor is in tune with the meanings of our words. In short, are we being genuinely, personally articulate?

When we sense a real link between how we converse privately and how we speak publicly, we're improving at both. We're becoming a natural. Our fear of losing face in either personal interactions or public speaking will diminish, and we'll be able to focus on our abilities without being overly self-conscious.

A colleague wisely taught public speaking by beginning

with interpersonal communication. He assigned college students to small groups in which they conversed about themselves and their communication fears and hopes.

He then asked students to attend public events and evaluate the speakers. Students discovered that there are no perfect speakers, and that a personal, genuine style is important. The students learned to be themselves by transitioning from personal conversations to public presentations.

Commendable communication is not so much about meeting the standards of well-known or impressive speakers as it is about becoming comfortably effective in our own skin. We best lead in tune with our growing maturity as persons. This is a hard lesson to learn, especially for hopeful leaders. We really don't have to impress others to be solid communicators—even as preachers.

Reflection

Are you comfortable with the way you communicate? Are others?

13

Conducting Triage

"In saying what I have in mind, will I really improve on the silence?" (OB, p. 305)

At the first meeting of a strategic-planning group, the facilitator asked us what we would like to accomplish. After others had spoken, I offered one word: "Wisdom."

Of course wisdom is a lofty goal. But it's also essential. The alternative is superficiality, often faddishness. Worse yet, foolishness.

Wisdom comes into view when we ask ourselves how we could truly serve the various stakeholders over the long run. What are we really in business for? How can we sagely carry that purpose forward?

For me, wisdom is not just an outcome, but also a criterion for judging our everyday actions. Seeking wisdom is a proactive means of avoiding rash communication resulting in slipshod decision-making.

Wisdom is a deep understanding of and discerning engagement with reality based on seasoned experience, shared common sense, well-rounded research, and attention to the interests of stakeholders. Without wisdom, our everyday communication tends toward superficial understandings.

We mistakenly tend to communicate compulsively. We don't dig deeper, patiently, to assess what we are actually communicating about—or should be communicating about. What really needs to be addressed? Why? How do we know? Most communication even about important matters is only surface deep.

I use the phrase "communicative triage" to capture the ongoing process of evaluating the relative significance of our various communication needs. Such triage is identifying and assessing the greatest communication-related needs (and opportunities) first, before the flood of immediate messaging swamps our minds and dilutes our interactions. When we do this before speaking, we are much more likely to improve upon the silence.

One of our essential communicative tasks as leaders is helping groups and organizations imagine and then articulate together wise decisions about their shared futures. We accept the fact that we can't communicate with everyone about everything. So we select words and phrases—and define them as needed—to diagnose conditions and subsequently to direct our thought, imagination, and action.

Communicative triage helps us take our language where it really needs to go. It leads us to ask and answer the essential questions about using our limited time, energy, and skills to serve others.

As leaders, we don't need to have all of the answers, but

we must responsibly nurture communicative triage. We lead partly by helping to keep first things first. We accept the calling to be trustees of the language an organization or group is using to define, share, and act upon its responsibilities. We are like doctors who, with the help of other staff and assessment technologies, perform regular checkups, not just emergency work.

A lack of communicative triage usually reflects laziness. Instead of regularly assessing our communication, we wait until problems arise that have to be addressed. We gradually fall into passive-aggressiveness. We come to realize that our communication no longer matches our job description.

Human communication naturally flows toward superficiality, disorganization, and dispersed self-interestedness. This communicative entropy threatens our relationships and the organizations that we serve.

Servant leaders steadily improve their communicative triage, minding the interests of stakeholders. They seek wisdom and make wise decisions. Their work itself is thereby strategic.

Reflection

Do you know which situations in your life and work most need your communicative attention? Are you taking enough time to determine how best to use your limited communicative resources?

14

Forestalling Busyness

"Busyness—compulsive busyness. Beneath the surface of much action, there is the drive to avoid the implications of growth."
(PS, p. 73)

In the early 2000s I spoke at a conference of information technologists. During my ballroom presentation the room lights were low and a spotlight focused on me. I couldn't see the audience well, but I could hear them keyboarding. I noted after a while that the timing of their clicking was not related to my speaking. I assumed they were probably working on email or other tasks.

I became increasingly frustrated. Was anyone actually listening to me present on the topic of communication?

So I stopped talking. I waited. And waited more. After a minute or so some of the clicking stopped.

Then I impatiently said something like this: "Okay, listen up. You invited me here to learn about communication. But I think many of you are not listening to me. If you need to work on your computers, please go to the lobby. The rest of us will continue."

I paused again. Within 30 seconds, complete silence. As far as I could tell, no one left the room.

The following week I received a fax from an attendee. It included a handwritten note that someone had passed around the room after my admonishment: "Does this guy [me] think we can't eat and listen, too?" The person who faxed me suggested that I didn't understand how well younger people could multitask. He had a point.

After thinking it over, however, I faxed back to him a note along these lines: "My older generation has a problem paying attention to one thing at a time. Your generation seems to have a problem paying attention to two or more things at a time. I'm not sure that's progress."

Research now shows that humans can't really multitask well at intellectual processes. We can't think carefully about two different things simultaneously. We can't really attend to a speaker and address email at the same time.

Heightened communicative busyness suffocates shared understanding. Instead of engaging carefully with one messenger, we scatter our thinking.

Our lives today are tornadic. Just to keep up with incessant messaging we succumb to considerable mental chaos. We become muddled message handlers, not communicators.

Moreover, we lose track of who we are, what we should rightly seek, and whom we should be like. Communicative chaos swamps personal integrity and right living.

In communication, more is not always better. Overload creates widening whirlpools of broken promises and distressed doggy paddlers. Unless we meticulously manage massive lists of communicative to-dos, we fail to do what we know we should. We disappoint ourselves as well as others.

Leadership communication requires focus, reflection, and an open, listening soul. Excessive busyness interferes with such communication. Communication takes patience—and more of it than what I demonstrated with the high-tech audience in Chicago.

Reflection

How busy are you with just receiving and transmitting messages? How much time do you actually spend reflecting on the quality of your relationships rather than just communicating within them?

15

Avoiding Gimmicks

A "gimmick" is "any organizational procedure that is
introduced with the hope of accomplishing what only better
leadership will do." (SS, p. 30)

While a student at the University of Illinois I regularly
walked past a small building that was scheduled to
house one giant superconducting computer. Vietnam War
protestors found out about the project and conducted demonstrations about the possible dire implications of high-
power computers for the growing military-industrial complex.

Today it is likely that every campus protestor carries a
smartphone more powerful than that massive unit that spark-
ed demonstrations a half century ago. Technological inno-
vators optimistically march forward in the face of critics'
concerns.

We need both champions and opponents of new technologies. Reality typically is located somewhere between the

viewpoints of extreme promoters and detractors. We humans are capable of stunning advances in tools and techniques, but we also tend to misuse even the most promising ones. Novel devices produce novel troubles, endlessly.

Most of us err on the side of technological exuberance. A major technology CEO excitedly called a new version of an existing product "epic." Epic?

We all tend to idolize the latest technologies as concrete signs of progress. We're never quite satisfied with existing gadgets. We're technologically restless, stirring for endless innovations. Few of us willingly let our cars, televisions, computers, and phones wear out. Obsolescence is more of a state of disappointment or jealousy than a matter of technological reality.

I believe that persistent technological enthusiasm extends beyond physical devices to language itself. We see words as powerful "techniques" that supposedly give us special control over others. Language, too, becomes faddish. We hope that the latest communication lingo will give us the power to transform our leadership.

Many top-selling business books are marketed on the basis of supposedly superior business "techniques." The hottest jargon about successful business practices symbolizes power. The language supposedly allows us to access secret methods that will purportedly revolutionize our leadership and guarantee career success. Special language is taken to be high-power technology.

No one of us is entirely immune to gimmicky language. We want to believe that there are easy-to-acquire physical devices and novel linguistic techniques that will clinch our professional success. Unresolved issues—technological and relational "glitches"—never fully disillusion us because we hear new techno-promises before the old ones are proved false.

We can't live without gadgets, but we can't always live well with them. So we have to make tough decisions about which technologies and what technological language are not just gimmicks. As servant leaders, we look out for the good of our stakeholders, not for technological advancement per se. We realize that knowing people must precede knowing techniques.

The same technologies that serve can enslave. The exuberant rhetoric about new technologies easily clouds our vision and makes it more difficult to make judicious decisions. Keeping up with innovation is not just about adopting emerging technologies. It's also about deciding when even extraordinary new devices can't sustain their attendant rhetoric in the midst of so many unsettling details, excessive costs, and unknown downsides. Our language about technological innovation doesn't change the underlying effects of technology.

Reflection

Do you overly value new communication technologies? For instance, do you fall into the trap of using technology as a substitute for in-person communication? Are you a sucker for the latest business or leadership lingo?

16

Embracing Diversity

"I found my way to people . . . whose perspectives were different from mine and who made me stretch." (PS, p. 275)

I was hired to help recruit a new faculty "person of color" for a small Southeast university. I worried that even if we found the ideal candidate in terms of professional background, research, and teaching abilities, the new professor might not fit well within the institution. To put it baldly, I feared that the university community wouldn't be particularly hospitable to someone who wasn't raised in the prevailing white, Anglo-Saxon, Protestant (WASP) culture.

The university eventually made an offer to a young Native-American PhD with sterling credentials who as an infant had been adopted by a WASP family. At least the professor looked like a person of color; certainly this would help the university admissions and marketing teams visually promote the school's commitment to diversity—an appealing marketing benefit. For all of its other benefits, diversity sells.

Ironically, the candidate for this position personally felt comfortable joining a WASPish faculty precisely because she would fit in fairly easily and would not be expected to act like a "real" person of color—whatever that meant.

In my view, diversity comes from the inside of people, not from the outside. Diversity has more to do with culture than color. Real diversity is experiential capacity.

Perhaps we servant leaders have to stretch beyond contemporary notions of diversity that are limited by simplistic categories. One easy test of whether or not someone will contribute to diversity is whether or not we will have difficulty communicating with him because of contrasting life experiences. If so, he probably represents actual diversity.

I suggest an expansive understanding of diversity based on cultural variations *across geographic space* (from place to place) and *through generational time* (from generation to generation). Variations in life experience always exist geographically and longitudinally.

For instance, every city is diverse across the various neighborhoods. An organization that fails to hire people from assorted neighborhoods misses out on resources that might represent different human experiences related to race, ethnicity, culture, religion, and the like.

From my space-and-time point of view, every organization already has some untapped diversity among its existing members—even among new hires who don't necessarily fit into popular diversity categories.

We also might discover that we ourselves personally provide diversity. We might have distinct life experiences based on where we were raised and the elders who nurtured us. We gain valuable life experiences from hardships as well as accomplishments.

Today one of our most severely self-imposed forms of centrism stems from a general cross-generational disinterest in the wisdom of the deceased. I find that I benefit immeasurably from my "communication" with wise persons who offer wisdom from the past. In a sense, I network with sages whose insights survive the test of time.

I placed at eye level in my home study two bookshelves of classic works on communication. I pick them up regularly and reread the sections I have marked up and notated. I also regularly consult them when I am preparing to write or speak. I want to keep alive my conversations with these wise writers. Their wisdom grows on me. Challenges me. Speaks to diversity beyond contemporary ideas. Their writings compel me to listen outside the here and now.

It seems to me that diversity requires deep communicative capacity. This capacity gains traction within organizations especially when leaders are personally hospitable to a wide range of other persons' life experiences. Diversity grows when people have the courage to listen beyond themselves and past simple, measurable categories of diversity that confine their understanding of reality.

Life experiences speak of the profound richness of human life—what nineteenth-century poet-priest Gerard Manley Hopkins called things that are "counter" (to expectations), and even wonderfully "strange."

Reflection

Do you value the diversity of others' life experiences enough that you willingly seek out contrary opinions?

17

Following Intuition

"Commitment to one's inner guidance is the consummate
achievement, but the line that separates that commitment
from fanaticism is fuzzy." (SL, p. 231)

I was on the first leg of a plane trip to be interviewed by a
board for a new job. It was an exciting career advancement
that would put me in regular contact with influential people.
My contact person from the board said that the job was mine
but that members wanted to meet and encourage me. The
interview would be friendly and affirming.

The problem was that I had been having major doubts
about taking the position. About moving my family. About
leaving behind many dear friends. About my ambition. And
more.

.Sitting quietly on the early-morning flight with the sunlight peeking over the horizon, reflecting, pondering, questioning my motives, I grew increasingly uneasy.

When I got off the plane to catch my connecting flight, I walked over to the nearest public phone (no cell phones then), called my board contact, and apologized. I would not be going to the interview. I just didn't feel right about moving ahead. He was understanding but astonished. I was as well. What in the world was I doing? I flew back home.

I have never really regretted that decision even though I don't know fully what was behind it. For me, the decision was more intuitive than deliberative. It just felt right in my heart.

I had discussed the position with some trusted friends. I had pondered it. But in the end I trusted a kind of inner instinct. I couldn't explain it—and I still can't. In the process of communicating with myself on that flight, I discovered that I lacked peace.

For me, inner guidance is essential in significant decision-making. As I understand it, intuitive decision-making is very different from purely emotional decision-making. I see intuition as the product of three potential relationships: (1) with ourselves, essentially through intrapersonal communication, (2) with trusted others, particularly close friends and colleagues, and for many (3) with a higher power I will simply call "God."

Intuition is generally defined in opposition to conscious reasoning. For me, conscious reasoning is part of intuition. For instance, when I am conversing with someone about a highly charged topic, I know from experience and reason that I should remain calm and listen carefully. Trying to confront someone about something that he is emotional about is not usually productive. Emotions are facts in and of themselves; they need to be considered, not challenged.

When I have time later in the day or early the following

morning, I will reflect on my conversations and relationships. I will try to think and feel empathetically without letting my own feelings immediately dictate how I might intuit my possible response. Often I will gain an intuitive sense of how to approach the topic and person the next time we meet. Usually I will then share my intuition with a trustworthy colleague. Does it sound right?

Intuitive communication is a soft, human practice. There is no logical place for intuition on a spreadsheet. I haven't figured out exactly how to teach it. Moreover, I can't explain why women seem to be more open to the value of intuition than are men. And older people more than younger ones.

Many servant leaders I know benefit from cultivating a sense of intuition as a means for understanding and working with others. The benefits include a greater internal sense of what it means to serve others rather than just to serve one's self or career. They also include higher-quality relationships in which people are more likely to flourish.

Finally, intuitive communication promotes internal peace. Perhaps those of us who cultivate intuition are less likely to do foolish things driven by negative personal feelings such as anger and resentment. Maybe, too, we have a creative edge because we don't limit decision making to quantitative information. I think so, intuitively. Thanks to such intuition, I still think I made the right decision on that plane years ago.

Reflection

Do you ever call upon intuition? Are you sure? Can you recall an example when it directly affected your communication?

18

Building Trust

"Legitimacy begins with trust." (SL, p. 70)

I was in Kentucky to visit a friend who was co-producing a television show on location. A company driver picked me up at the airport and began chatting about local lore as we drove through the mountains to the set. I was enjoying the ride.

I asked him what it was like for him as a rural Kentuckian to work for high-level Hollywood people. "Well," he said, "the one producer out here is great. He's become a friend. I love talking with him. I'd do anything for him."

Then he spoke about the other producer. "You know, that guy is so full of himself nobody around here trusts him."

I was stunned. Then he added, "The next time that guy comes out here I might just drive him out into the country and toss him out of the van. Let him leg it back to town."

Two producers. Only one is liked and trusted. Fortunately that was my producer friend. I sighed in relief.

Mutual trust is vital for human communication. But building trust is a slow, delicate dance in which partners learn to lead and follow toward ever-deeper confidence in one another. Trust is hard to earn and easy to lose. One lie can destroy trust. So can routine flattery.

Duplicity is deadly. Two-faced persons who dishonestly compliment others are treacherous. They sow dissension while giving the impression that they are true friends. When called on their deceitfulness, they tend to be quick to blame others, slow to forgive, slower to apologize, and slowest yet to make heartfelt amends.

More than any other virtue, trustworthiness establishes a leader's communicative legitimacy. Trust is the platform for colleagues to listen to each other and to express themselves openly.

When we enter into relationships, we cautiously seek trust. When we work with those we can trust, we don't have to invest precious time fretting about what we say. We can flourish within a community of servant friends. This is a vision of community worth painting.

Organizations require trust at all levels. Can interviewers and interviewees trust one another? Can entry-level employees trust colleagues and supervisory personnel? Can middle managers trust those competing for the same higher positions? Can public relations staff trust what management and trustees say about the organization? Can stockholders trust the material in annual reports?

I customarily checked directly with a higher-level supervisor when an immediate manager-leader would tell me something that I suspected was untrue. I realized that if I automatically accepted intuitively questionable interpretations of what people said or did, I could become a carrier of damaging falsehoods. Moreover, though questionable, such messages would nevertheless color my view of the person referred to in the messages.

If a questionable, work-related message was a comment about a particular person, I would find a way naturally—at the right time and place—to ask that person about it without mentioning the source. And I tried to stay away from gossipers at settings in which they were prone to operate, such as social gatherings overly lubricated with alcohol.

My Hollywood producer friend devised a strategy to head off distrust during production. At the first meeting on the set he asked everyone to follow one simple rule: "If anything goes wrong, ask yourselves only one question: 'How can we fix it?' Let's never blame anyone. That will only interfere with our ability to come together to make this a great production worthy of an audience."

Mutual honesty and respect build confidence. Confidence, in turn, nurtures trust. If we work with trustworthy coworkers, we are fortunate. If they are also the kinds of virtuous people who are willing to respectfully challenge our trustworthiness, we are doubly fortunate.

Trust-filled leaders lift an organization. If our top leaders demonstrate integrity that earns the trust of the various stakeholders, we will aim to be trustworthy followers. We will find ourselves encircled by persons who are worth following regardless of their official positions above or below us.

Reflection

Are you fully worthy of everyone's trust? Whom should you

ask to verify your trustworthiness? Who knows the true you besides your family members?

19

Cultivating Friendship

"A friend called to tell me that he had just been made head of
a philanthropic foundation. . . . My immediate response . . .
was, 'The first thing that will happen to you is that you will
no longer know who your friends are.'" (PS, 47–48)

I was at a critical point professionally. I was going to be
fired.

Because of some of my personal convictions, I had become an emotional threat to a high-level manager that I
barely knew. I had no power or authority to do anything
about it. An emotionally disturbed but extremely influential
person was crushing me.

I was relatively young and foolish, simmering in anger. In
my daydreams, I imagined confronting this person, winning
an argument, and forcing him to resign. But in my nighttime
dreams I always lost the fight. My imagination retold a tragic
tale of my woe.

Challenging the honesty of a powerful leader when you don't have much of a case other than "he said that she said" is not the way to make friends in high places.

But when I shared my doomsday scenario with a higher-placed co-worker, he took a personal interest. I think he was motivated by empathy and a strong sense of justice. He asked me to keep silent about the situation and promised to look into it for me.

Eventually my friend courageously took my side, privately approached the villain, and put his own job on the line. It was two against one. And it was no longer just a personal issue related to my accuser and me.

My friend was a true friend. He trusted me. He took on my struggle. He advocated for me bravely, knowing that he might face consequences. To this day I am still stunned by that turn of events in my professional life. Whenever I recall it, I am filled with wonder, culminating in gratitude. I ponder whether I ever could be such a self-sacrificial colleague.

A true friend is a servant in heart, mind, and action. She listens to another's heartbeat in the messy matters of life and work. This empathetic friend accepts another's thoughts and emotions without judgment. Then such a friend can begin to do whatever is best for the other person: advocacy, admonishment, encouragement, and the like. Two such mutual friends experience solidarity anchored in truth and love.

Friends become compassionate stewards of each other's flourishing. The servant-friend carries another's burdens, like serving jail time for him. She shares in another's joy and delight, like being a matron of honor at a wedding. The two journey together, keeping each other on the path to ever-greater appreciation and ever-deeper service.

I have had a handful of such friends in my professional life. The friendships started naturally, through a mutual affinity. Eventually I discovered that I had to invest more into each friendship for it to grow. I had to commit myself to being the kind of friend that I would like to have, and then to deliberately act upon my personal commitment to the relationship. At work, the result in each case was not only a growing friendship, but more enjoyable and meaningful work.

Having at least two friends of this kind in an organization makes all of the difference between being eager to serve and simply desiring to go to work to pay the bills. We can handle much more professional uncertainty, stress, and confusion when we are communing with friends along the way.

Our friends give us heart. We give them heart. Together we become heart-to-heart friends.

Today professionalism carries dry and stoic connotations. We think of professionals as people who pursue dispassionate skillfulness. Having fun, even enjoying work, seems rather unprofessional.

By contrast, a servant leader experiences intrinsic delight from working for and with like-hearted friends. The most satisfying work involves a community of friends.

Friendship is the highest form of community even within professions. By delighting in serving each other, friends sow evocative collegiality. Friends point everyone to a soul-satisfying professionalism. My career-saving friend was such a true professional.

Reflection

Can you identify just a few colleagues who are true, mutual

friends? Be sure to tell them in person that you appreciate their friendship. Give thanks for them.

20

Challenging Self-Deception

"By the time we reach maturity, we have a vast amount of
experience stored away that effectively conditions perception
and sometimes will not permit us to perceive correctly."
(OB, p. 35)

My college students and I developed an effective way of
generating engaging class discussions. We would find
people online who were producing thought-provoking videos
about communication. Then we would invite the producers
to discuss their work via live video with the class.

Most of the videos were produced by nonacademic,
nonprofessional, self-educated amateurs who loved the topic.
These class guests were amazingly articulate, informed, and
balanced during class discussion. They were unacknowledged
but wise experts. They challenged my assumptions about the
need for formal education in communication.

We all view reality through preconceived notions that
may or may not be accurate. There are many types of
"correctness"—socially acceptable, unquestioned assumptions. There are liberal and conservative ideologies, academic

and popular theories, religious traditions, shared ethnic and racial experiences, best-seller lists, and much more.

We humans are subjective creatures. We tend to think others are wrong and we are correct. We even surround ourselves with like-minded persons to reinforce our correctness.

Moreover, as we simplify our assumed understanding of reality, we reject ideas and data that don't sustain our prejudices. We naturally affirm facts, beliefs, and opinions that we already hold. We laud similarly minded, alleged experts. We thereby propagandize ourselves.

The challenge for servant leaders is twofold: (1) to identify our own assumptions, and (2) to engage persons that hold contrasting views. These two challenges—*honest self-knowledge* and *discomforting social interaction*—can reduce self-propaganda.

In order to confront our own self-propaganda, we have to listen charitably to those with whom we seemingly disagree. We have to listen outside of our emotional and intellectual comfort zones. We have to assume that others could be right and that we might be partly or fully wrong. Over time we will become humbler and more self-critical.

I've learned that being a professor is an extraordinary opportunity and an intimidating responsibility. The greatest opportunity is co-learning with students as a community of curiosity. My students and I together could uncover valuable, practical, and counterintuitive truths about human communication; it was inspiring.

But some days I wondered if I was the greatest challenge to student learning. Was I adequately open to personal enlightenment? Was I above my own self-propaganda? My professorial title and academic degrees were insufficient for protecting myself from self-delusion. Sometimes they were ego-feeding stumbling blocks to intellectual growth. I was my own enemy.

Reflection

What do you know about yourself in your heart that you have been unwilling to address with your mind? Are you excessively ideological or one sided in your views of reality? Can you accept the fact that you have much to learn—including from people with far less professional status?

21

Practicing Fittingness

"So much of caring depends upon knowing and interacting with persons in the intimacy of propinquity." (PS, p. 22)

During a sabbatical in Florida, I visited different churches to see how they used communication technology. I discovered that many faith groups employed video projections of everything from announcements and Scripture to sermon outlines, Holy Land maps, congregational photos, song lyrics, promotional videos, and images of clouds, mountains, sunlight, palm trees, beaches, and tropical flowers.

One PowerPoint-styled presentation included animation and sound effects every time the preacher moved to the next bullet point on his projected sermon outline. People in seats ahead of me delightedly jabbed each other in the ribs each time a new visual effect hit the screen. I was astonished.

I concluded that many church presentations lacked *fittingness*—the proper fit of medium with message. Some churches failed to use the technology appropriately for worship. Worship is worship. It has its own, honored purpose—just as entertainment has a function in life. PowerPoint is a technological medium, not a purpose. Not all uses of PowerPoint are fitting for all purposes, including worship.

When used wisely, a technology can enhance communication. But not all uses of all media equally fit all communication purposes. Is it fitting to discuss a job-performance review on the phone? Via email? When and why?

Leaders daily face dozens of different communication purposes, from encouraging colleagues to training people, and from painting a vision to listening to critics. Which media shall we use for each of the many purposes? Email? A phone call? Live video? A handwritten note? A public speech? An in-person conversation? Which medium is the best fit?

Suppose a leader has to lay off someone. What is the most fitting medium? Why? Is a letter fitting? If so, how should it be delivered? What about email? A text message? An in-person meeting—maybe with an exit interview? Is the goal simply to fire someone—in which case a Dear "X" letter or email could work—or is it to humanely end a relationship for the betterment of both parties?

The basic purpose of our communication should point us toward the most fitting medium. Of course the most fitting medium might not always be the most efficient in terms of time and cost. Trade-offs are inevitable.

When we fit the medium with the message, we gain communicative traction. Leaders who don't take fittingness into account lose traction by increasing misunderstanding.

Determining proper fit is not easy, partly because we use

the same language to describe machines and people—input, output, memory, smart, intelligent, and the like. We live in a high-tech culture that equates messaging with communication, and bandwidth with meaning.

I don't really care about my cell phone's processing power or my computer screen's resolution so long as I can easily use the technologies to communicate well with others. I want to use relatively transparent media that have the capacity required for a given purpose.

If my means—my technologies—become my ends, I'm in communicative trouble. I'm chasing after machines when I need to be attending to people.

New information technologies will not magically make us better communicators. In the end they reflect back to us the values we put into their development and use. In other words, we become like the communication technologies we venerate.

Using a medium to its intrinsic capacity is an art, easily lost. When I compose a handwritten note, perhaps I am doing my part by example to keep alive that simple but effective means for others to use and enjoy. Servant leaders, it seems to me, ought to be so inclined or we will all lose some of the capacity to employ older media well, and miss out on opportunities to expand the otherwise invisible capacity in new media.

Reflection

When was the last time you remember using the wrong medium for a particular purpose? What would you have done differently?

22

Timing Dialogue

"There are moments that contain eternity." (SL, p. 300)

I found myself in the middle of a heated board meeting at a private school. The issue was whether or not the board should hire an additional teacher in order to reduce the excessive third-grade class sizes. The administrator opposed a new hire. Parents supported it.

The dialogue intensified. I wondered if I could add anything valuable to the discourse.

Eventually comments trailed off. There wasn't much new to be said. It was a classic standstill. No one seemed happy. Yet no one seemed ready to leave. There we all sat.

Then I stood up.

"I'm grateful to be here with you all tonight," I began. "I'm heartened by the turnout. I'm thankful for your candor. I'm truly grateful that we all care enough to come together to try to tackle this issue on behalf of our children and school."

I paused.

Then I faced the school administrator. "We trust you, but many of us fear next year. I do. We just need to be assured that we will have a plan in place that will serve our students, our children."

I continued, "I would suggest that you put together a specific proposal without the full cost of hiring another teacher. Tell us what will work, why it will work, how you will make it work, and what it will actually cost compared with hiring a teacher."

I concluded, "I'm sure everyone here will review it carefully, and we can meet again as needed to discuss it. We all care about our students, and that's something we don't want to lose."

I sat down. I could feel the tension leaving the room. At least it was leaving me. There was more silence, but it was good silence. My suggested plan soon moved forward.

I probably didn't speak that eloquently. I did try to speak from the heart on behalf of everyone in the room. And I spoke positively. I knew that we all wanted a way out of the impasse. I believed that there was still good faith. Someone needed to tap into it before the meeting ended. I felt called.

A crucial aspect of communicative leadership is timing. In this case, if I had tried to say the same thing before attendees had voiced their feelings, the tension probably would have continued to escalate anyway.

People receive in their hearts only what they're ready to receive, when they are ready to receive it. Our task is to sense when they are ready.

In communication, timing is not everything but it can be critically important. The same things could be said at multiple times and be successful only in one of them. This fact can be baffling and sobering.

In the Western world we tend to think of time in terms of scheduling. We focus so much on scheduling that we miss opportunities to seize unplanned moments.

The ancient Greeks had two words for time—*chronos* and *kairos* ("kye-ros"). The former was sequential time. The latter meant the right or opportune time. We seem to be losing a sense of the latter.

Kairos is the right time, neither too soon nor too late. Kairos, as I'm using it, means the right moment to serve in a particular way—including to speak up or to remain silent. What directs a person to seize such a moment is wisdom, and sometimes intuition, or both.

The key is for us to be available in the present to see the possibilities for serving others and ourselves. We are free to say what should be said when it should be said, to listen when listening is most needed, and to be open to communication beyond our schedules and apparent abilities.

Some communication situations beg for *kairos*. For instance, deciding when and how to offer forgiveness always has something to do with *kairos*, when both hearts are open.

At the school board meeting I had no prepared remarks. I just wanted to be there, available, to be as responsible as I could. In a sense, the moment seized me. The timing was right. My words served those present. The board later settled on a one-year plan that included more aides and volunteers.

Perhaps, as Robert Greenleaf speculates about timing, there was a dash of eternity in those moments toward the meeting's end. In any case, I experienced *kairos*, and with it gratitude.

Reflection

Can you recall a situation where your own or others' communication included a dash of *kairos*? What might you now learn from those situations?

23

Engaging Conflict

"The well-being of the other person may depend on a constructive tension that I may be able to create; therefore, I must weigh my responsibility for saying the words or taking the actions that will bring this tension about." (OB, p. 48)

Some years ago other investors and I sold a company to a much larger corporation with international financing. Since we traded most of our ownership for stock in the larger company, we keenly watched its progress. We heard that the board of the larger company might eventually take it public.

The new management spent lavishly on itself, taking the company from profit to debt. Soon some shareholders asked me to intervene with the new management. I reluctantly agreed. My job was to create some healthy conflict toward a good resolution.

I have never liked conflict. I grew up amidst so much emotional turmoil that I learned creative ways to circumvent it. Avoidance became an art form for me.

But I eventually learned that wisely instigated conflict could be the most productive route to improved relationships, greater personal peace, and even professional success. How people employ, address, and sometimes resolve conflict are critically important. Conflict, I learned, is an intellectual or emotional resource in waiting.

In nonphysical conflicts we might strike one another with words or with silence. Sometimes such conflicts result in false truces where participants cease communication altogether; silence becomes an emotional weapon.

When I visited company management, they nodded heads and smiled. They gave me a pleasant tour, introduced me around, catered a delicious lunch, and shook my hand on my way out the door. I was to be humored, not engaged. I couldn't seem to generate any needed conflict.

The keys to using conflict positively are *depersonalizing*, *empathizing*, and *maintaining dialogue*. First, we depersonalize conflict by focusing on the substantive matters of disagreement rather than on the personalities involved.

Second, we empathize with others. Their feelings are facts. Are they hurt, fearful, cynical, hopeful, frustrated, or excited? Conflicts occur in the context of people's emotions, not just their reasoning. If others see that we truly empathize with them—that we understand, acknowledge, accept, and identify with their life experiences—they will more likely trust us in substantive discussion.

Third, substantive conflict is most productive when nurtured over time in ongoing dialogue. People need time to understand and engage each other. They need to become comfortable with each other's views and conclusions—and with potential compromise and consensus.

Engaging conflict is a process, not an outcome. I should have developed relationships with management before meeting with them. I should have discerned in advance their feelings. And I should have kept the dialogue going with multiple visits. I failed.

Reflection

How do you address conflict? How high is your tolerance for engaging in emotionally charged conversations?

24

Fostering Compromise

"Compromise makes life on this earth possible, with normal human beings living in relative freedom." (OB, p. 49)

A group of U.S. Congresspersons told me privately how essential compromise is for national politics. They said their work would grind to a halt without compromise. It was a sobering discussion.

Some people feel that compromise is unethical. For them, to compromise is to act against their convictions, to sell out.

It helps to think of compromise (com-promise) in terms of making "common promises" beyond our self-interest.

For instance, spouses compromise in order to respect individual differences, reduce unnecessary conflict, and nurture a healthier marriage. Couples take marriage vows; they promise to serve each other rather than just themselves. Such promises should lead to compromises for the good of the marriage.

The best compromises respect individual differences while seeking mutually satisfactory outcomes. Compromise is a way for us as imperfect people to affirm our differences and yet act and live together peacefully. Compromise is realistic, not flawless. Sometimes it's the best option. Sometimes it's even a wonderful option.

The process of compromising requires careful interaction. The parties involved have to aim for a mutually acceptable outcome amidst their potentially divisive interests, communicative styles and claims. How someone says something can be just as important as what he says. Mutual respect is essential.

One key is finding out what people really want, not just what they say they want. Emotions always underlie negotiations. As I said earlier, feelings are facts; they need to be addressed. We all are emotional as well as rational persons.

Nevertheless, compromise-directed communication has to address participants' *nonnegotiables*—what they are logically or emotionally unwilling to give up. What do they most cherish? What do they feel that they most need—and maybe that they can't live without? Security? Respect? Fairness? Tangibles?

When people suggest that compromise is selling out, they are usually referring to what they perceive for themselves as nonnegotiables. For instance, many people include moral or religious convictions in their list of personal nonnegotiables.

I hold some convictions that I will not act against. I have quietly turned down work over them. I have graciously ended relationships because of them. Others have terminated relationships with me over them. To compromise on my basic convictions would unravel the tapestry of my heart. I would lose my inner integrity.

If we can't articulate our own nonnegotiables, we probably will unwittingly compromise our integrity. We need to know ourselves well.

When we act against our convictions, we undermine our self-regard. We put expediency ahead of integrity. Over time, such compromise can turn us into communicative chameleons. We end up pretending we are different persons in different situations and with different people.

As leaders, we have obligations beyond ourselves. What do our organizations profess? What are the nonnegotiables represented in their vision and mission statements? How should nonnegotiables direct organizations' negotiations on behalf of various shareholders? What are acceptable and unacceptable compromises for others in our organization—not just for us?

We all must make tough personal decisions about what we can and can't promise. If we promise only what we can sincerely affirm, we will not sell our souls. Compromise is all about such healthy promises.

Reflection

Does it help you to see compromise as mutually satisfactory promises in an imperfect world? Is there anything that you personally need to compromise about—without violating your nonnegotiable values and beliefs?

25

Seeking a Prophetic Voice

"The prophet brings vision and penetrating insight."
(PS, p. 120)

Near the height of the dot-com craze I was asked to respond to a presentation by a leader from a large Silicon Valley consulting firm. He combined an impressive slide presentation and a well-rehearsed speech into an awe-inspiring, almost worshipful event. His basic message was that digital technologies would revolutionize everything. No matter what the human problem, technological salvation was at hand.

When the consultant finished, the crowd roared with approval to a standing ovation. The presenter then left.

It was my turn to speak.

"Okay, you've just heard proclamations from the heavenly realm. Now I want equal time. I represent the devil." I heard a few chuckles. "Isn't the devil in the details?"

Using historical examples, I explained that new communication technologies never fully live up to the hype surrounding their emergence. The bad comes with the good. Some problems get solved and new ones emerge. Financial, social, and organizational costs are always greater than the predictions. The devil is indeed in the details. Technological life is more like purgatory than heaven.

I added that most of our communication should focus on everyday needs such as speaking and listening well, explaining thoroughly, persuading respectfully, and building consensus or compromise. Communication technologies cannot guarantee we will do these well. And they can complicate as well as enhance our work toward shared understanding.

No matter how much technology we use, the natural movement of communication is toward entropy, not organization. Used foolishly, technology tends to fragment our relationships. New technologies cannot revolutionize human nature.

Fortunately, "prophets" come along and challenge our technological assumptions—especially our overly optimistic rhetoric. They provide a needed dose of reality.

A communicative prophet is not so much a prognosticator as an interrogator. The prophet asks the tough, missing, or counterintuitive questions. The prophet also recalls history and cautions us about reading too much into the future.

We servant leaders need prophetic critiques of communication within organizations. We need people who are able to identify what we are saying and how it does or doesn't comport with reality. In short, we need great listeners and counterintuitive thinkers who will challenge us to consider the gap between our rhetoric and reality.

How prophets deliver their challenges is extremely important. Often a humble sense of humor is essential. So is critiquing principles rather than criticizing specific people.

All prophetic communication itself needs to be examined. It might be self-propaganda. It might be partly wrong. It might be true but not really penetrating. Examining surface language is never sufficient. What is the underlying story— the subtext? How do we know for sure?

Such prophets can help keep us honest. If something sounds or looks too good to be true, it probably is. If everyone seems to agree outwardly but many people seem to be unhappy, something is wrong. Who will speak up?

Reflection

Do you recall a time when you had special insight while attending a meeting, listening to a speaker, or conversing with a colleague? Did you speak up? Are you willing to speak up responsibly and appropriately if you find that surface rhetoric is inaccurate or incomplete—especially rhetoric about communication?

26

Employing Good Humor

"The relevance of humor to growth in responsibility is that
we can have this loving, indulgent inward smile about
ourselves—self-acceptance, some call it." (SL, 302)

One of the most gifted communicators I have known
was Jean Shepherd, who wrote the film *A Christmas
Story*, about the young Ralphie who desperately wants a Red
Ryder BB Gun for Christmas. Perhaps the most significant
thing Shepherd taught me was his understanding of humor.

According to Shepherd, the best humor derives primarily
from ironic grace. In his stories, characters survive a series of
everyday minitragedies, some of which are of their own,
ironic making.

From this perspective, humor helps us all realize that
although the world is a maze, we can find our ways through it
just as others before us have done. A humorous tale says to
us, "You too have lived—and survived—everyday life."

Humor better equips us to live, grow, and celebrate together our shared human condition.

In this bigger context, even life's seemingly minor events and people's ordinary foibles are grace-touched. Jerry Seinfeld, whom Shepherd influenced, based *Seinfeld* largely on this type of humor. The show that some people said was "about nothing" was, in my view, actually a series of hopeful tales about everyday human foibles and inexplicable grace.

A servant leader will discover that humor is one of her greatest communicative assets. We need to be everyday storytellers who can gather others to hear about organizations' and individuals' run-of-the-mill minitragedies that nevertheless point to grace.

A servant leader sets the right narrative tone by first capturing his own mistakes—such as losing his temper (as Ralphie does with the bully), failing to listen to reasonable warnings ("You'll shoot your eye out"), and being hypocritical (Ralphie has to suck on a soap bar for uttering a word that his father, the "Old Man," has used frequently and forever).

Such a personal sense of humor grows from hope-giving humility, a down-to-earth-ness (closeness to the *humus*) that keeps a leader grounded in honest self-criticism, warm self-acceptance, and steadfast self-improvement. With this attitude in mind, a leader can begin sharing other persons' stories compassionately and hopefully.

By telling such humorous stories, a servant leader says to everyone, "We've all been there. We're all going to make it. We all know that the journey will be fun as well as frustrating."

Leaders who cannot humbly empathize with followers

tend to be arrogant. Václav Havel, the dissident playwright who became the first Czech Republic president after the fall of the Berlin Wall, writes in *The Art of the Impossible*, "The man who hates . . . is incapable of making a joke, only of bitter ridicule; he can't be genuinely ironic because he can't be ironic about himself."

Havel admits, "The lower I am, the more proper my place seems; and the higher I am, the stronger my suspicion is that there has been some mistake."

Humorless leaders love to criticize everyone but themselves. They can't handle criticism because they consider themselves above the fray, grander than the rest of humanity.

There is at least a tinge of that arrogance in all of us. We servant leaders know this is the case because we have nearly "shot our eyes out" on numerous occasions. Fortunately, we lived to tell the story with grace and hope.

Reflection

Do you have a real sense of humor tinged with grace? Do you use jokes to put others down and make yourself feel better— or to address common human foibles and build up shared hope?

27

Crafting Artfully

"Communicate ideas that give hope and in language that is powerful and beautiful, words that lift the spirit." (PS, p. 228)

I required my public-speaking students to evaluate public presentations by well-known campus guests. Students discovered that the most engaging presenters delight audiences by expressing themselves artfully.

The artistic aspects of communication are important in much of our everyday discourse, from our emails to conversations and memos. Yet we tend to overlook the artistic—or "aesthetic"—quality of our aural, textual, and visual messages.

We usually think of communication only in terms of conveying practical information. Sometimes all that we need to communicate is straight-up information. But much of our communication is relational, not just informational; it's communication that is meant to persuade, motivate, encourage, and the like. Too much of even such relational communication is drab, uninteresting, and uninspiring.

The ancient Roman orator Cicero suggested that great human communication should delight. Delight: give joy.

When we communicate beyond mere information, do we give delight? Do others enjoy reading or hearing our messages—even if they don't agree with us? Do we even think about the creative aspects of our conversations, speeches, presentations, memos, blogs, and photos? Not all the time. Certainly not compulsively. But regularly, as appropriate?

One CEO regularly sent me relationally dead emails. Most emails were three or four terse sentences. I felt like I was being barked at, not being related to: "Do this, do that, consider this, what about that, bark, bark, bark." The messages were short but not sweet. I found little delight in receiving them. There was no personality, no style in them; machines could have manufactured them.

A leader who creates fewer messages but attends more artfully to each one will gain interested audiences, build stronger relationships, and ultimately become a better servant.

The three artistic elements that I find most helpful are *unity*, *variety*, and *intensity*.

Unity is simply oneness of content and purpose; as I use it, unity includes coherence—making sure that the content "sticks together." A speech, email, video, memo, presentation, planned conversation, and the like should be organized around one or a few closely related themes. It should not stray. The root meaning of "art" in Latin gets at the concept of joining or fitting together.

Variety in communication is the range of expressiveness—the various ways the communicator interestingly expresses ideas, relates ideas to other ideas, and employs a range of engaging examples or illustrations. I often think of variety as the opposite of boring repetitiveness and tiresome predictability.

A PowerPoint presentation that employs the identical number of bullet points on every slide or even uses only bulleted text will come across as unimaginative, as purely informational; after three or four slides most viewers will stop reflecting on the presentational content.

Intensity is the overall level of emotional or intellectual impact on the audience. The communicator's own passion needs to touch recipients. Uninspired communicators lack intensity. Of course intensity can be excessive or inappropriate. Still, messages that don't connect with others' hearts are not likely to achieve intended goals.

Every message we create is more or less a work of art. The quality of a message depends partly on how well it conveys the speaker's intention with unity, variety, and intensity.

We humans are artistic creatures; everything we do has an artistic dimension. The sheer effectiveness of our communication depends partly on how well we appropriately delight others. Our relational form and informational content need to embrace each other.

Reflection

When you have time, do you think about your own communication as art? Do you compose your messages to make them more delightful for others?

28

Mentoring Others

"But the greatest foresight, the most difficult and most exciting, is the influence one wields on the future by helping the growth of people who will be in commanding positions in the next generation." (OB, p. 79)

When my son was about five years old we began a tradition of walking around the neighborhood after dinner. As he grew older we had some amazing conversations. We talked about hopes and fears. About doing what is right. About what it's like to be a professor and a boy. About relatives, neighbors, and friends.

I didn't know it at the time, but I was learning—vicariously through my son's feedback—how to mentor.

About two decades later, having dedicated much of my life to teaching, writing, speaking, and consulting, I realized that I was spending about 20 percent of my time mentoring even though I had never really sought to become a mentor. It just happened. I now believe that mentoring is essential.

In my view, mentoring is sharing a journey. It requires mutual honesty and deep listening. A mentor sometimes points the way ahead but is not primarily a career coach. Mentors and mentees serve each other well by sharing their own journeys of service to others.

Effective mentors ask themselves the same questions they ask their mentees: Where have you been? Where are you now? Where do you think you should be headed—and why?

A related, revealing question is this: are you being honest with yourself about your journey? Mentors and mentees wander when they try to plan the future without honestly taking stock of the past and present.

Numerous mentees have disappeared from my life after I requested candor. Knowing that such a query can seem disrespectful, I do soften it as appropriate: "Are you sure?" "What is your conscience or your heart telling you?" I've learned that I have to remain somewhat skeptical of mentees just as I have to be skeptical about myself.

Over the years I developed an acronym to help mentees look for solid mentors, and to assist mentors in truthfully considering how qualified they are to take on mentees: AWE, standing for *accountability*, *wisdom*, and *experience*.

Accountability is essential. Honesty and accountability go hand in hand.

I once had to tell a mentor about something I had done that was quite dishonest. He was angry as well as compassionate. While holding me accountable, he walked with me through that mess. He affirmed my humanness by traveling with me through that dark valley.

As I suggested earlier, wisdom is the kind of practical

knowledge gained from life experience; wisdom is deep knowledge that has proven to lead us to proper action—to do what we should do in varied, complicated situations. A phrase such as "Speak only if you can improve upon the silence" is practical wisdom. Wisdom doesn't guarantee professional success; it fosters authentic professionalism. A mentor can help us identify, understand, and apply wisdom.

Finally, a worthy mentor offers a mentee experience. The mentor more or less has "been there" as a follower and eventually a leader. The mentor knows what the journey is like, even what to expect on the road ahead.

On the evening before my son was to be wed, he knocked on my hotel door and asked if I wanted to go for a walk. We journeyed together silently through the streets of old Charleston, South Carolina.

Eventually he asked me how I felt the night before his mother and I were married. We shared notes about our respective monumental nights. To be invited to that conversation was one of the most rewarding experiences of my fatherly career. We shared our stories, and I realized that my mentee was becoming one of my mentors as we journeyed together in unpretentious awe.

Reflection

Are you ready to venture out of your own complacency and to journey with someone you hold in AWE? Have you identified anyone for that role?

29

Affirming Hope

"I am hopeful for these times, despite the tension and conflict, because more natural servants are trying to see clearly the world as it is and are listening carefully to prophetic voices that are speaking *now*." (SL, p. 9)

I rarely post photos on social media. When our first grandchild was born, however, I had an experience that temporarily changed my mind.

I was visiting our daughter and son-in-law shortly after they arrived home from the hospital with their new son. As my grandson fell asleep in my arms, I gave thanks in my heart and pondered his future, filled with hope.

Soon my daughter took a photo of the new grandson and me quietly resting on the sofa—the two of us at peace. I posted that photo online with a short note about hope.

Every new relationship is a setting for building hope. It could be a relationship with a new colleague. A new intern. A new mentor or mentee. A new friend and collaborator. A new teacher or student. A new child or grandchild.

From an initial handshake or hug to a goodbye kiss in a hospital or home, much of our communication carries a sense of beginnings and endings. Hope is perhaps the deepest emotion that links together the past, present, and future.

We tell stories of the past as parables of the future. "Remember when . . ." Such hope nurtures the human spirit even in the face of always-present disappointment and despair.

A servant leader accepts responsibility for helping to keep hope alive in daily discourse. Hope probably is an essential intangible for leading. Every human being needs hope in order to keep working in the face of challenges.

The most difficult aspect of communicating hope is appraising it suitably. As with flattery, overdone expressions of hope implode. The meaning caves in on itself.

Perhaps the opposite of hopeful communication is resentful communication. Hope assumes that what one wants is likely to happen; it is projected goodness. Resentment assumes that the past will dictate the future; it focuses on previously unmet desires, and so it projects disappointment. Whenever we feel or express resentment, we pass along unresolved grievances. We keep alive bitterness and anger. We suffocate hope.

An administrative colleague used to start meetings by asking attendees for "Good News." What had attendees accomplished lately? What positive feedback had they received? What were they grateful for? The answers gave us hope.

At our finest, we awake each day expectantly. We do the best we can under the circumstances. We release all pretenses of perfection and superiority. We whisper to ourselves the serenity prayer: "God, grant me the serenity to accept the things I cannot change, courage to change the things I can, and wisdom to know the difference."

Holding my new grandson filled me with the kind of hope that still inspires me to serve others. Sharing hope gives hope.

Reflection

What gives you hope? What takes away from your hope?

30

Living a Legacy

"Is not every servant a leader because of influence by
example?" (SL, p. 329)

For me, one of the most sobering aspects of parenting was
discovering that my children were becoming like me. No
matter what I intentionally taught my children, they also picked up on how I lived—the good and the bad.

We humans "speak" and "listen" with our whole lives.
We imitate each other for years, decades, and even generations.

Of course we also critique each other along the way.
Colleagues monitor us, interpreting our feelings toward them,
judging our actions, discerning what we value and devalue,
observing what delights and angers us, and much more.

As our relationships grow, our lives become changing
tapestries that we hang on the wall daily for friends, family,
and colleagues to see and to selectively weave into their own

lives. All of our intended communication occurs in the context of our broader lives as living messages.

We leaders establish legacies that impact others during and after our lives. We imitate others; others imitate us. We teach and we model. We intentionally and unintentionally influence by how we lead and how we live. We all mentor, if only by example.

Being an intentional servant leader creates a life worth imitating. We don't have to be perfect leaders to establish a worthy legacy. Instead, we just need to engage our hearts and our minds to the best of our abilities, with excellence and compassion, in the service of others. Observers will have a chance to discover a fine way to live. Our lives will speak well of the joy of being a servant first, and a leader second.

Today the word "legacy" typically denotes a passing along of money or property to the next generation. In older usage, a legacy was also a type of mission on which a ruler sent an ambassador to a group of people. The ambassador had authority to act on behalf of the sender and for the benefit of the recipients.

Thus the ambassador him- or herself became a leader, by serving a particular group. The deputized leader acted as a diplomatic ambassador *for* a home people and *to* another people. The ambassador "bequeathed" a legacy to those he was called to serve.

Today, a servant leader can be an ambassador bearing a legacy. The leader's mentors and community—all from whom the leader has learned how to be a good servant—have given the leader a mission: to be a servant worthy of imitation.

I've learned over the years that my professional books,

lectures, mentoring, and consulting are only part of my gift to future generations. My life is the primary gift. How I live, in all of my relationships and roles, sets the real, enduring value of my gift to future generations. This is a sobering truth.

A practical symbol helps me remember. My daughter and son-in-law gave me a special pen. It's handcrafted of wood, essentially one of a kind. I carry it religiously. Every time I put it in my pocket, take it out, and write with it, I am reminded that what I write and, indeed, how I live are parts of my legacy. I need to watch what I write, and make right how I live. Others are reading my prose, listening to my speech, and observing my actions. The pen helps me attend responsibly to my life's legacy.

Reflection

Do you see yourself as a servant? Do you see communication as a gift for serving others? In short, are you ready to live your life as a message of legacy?

About the Author

After growing up in Chicago, Quentin J. Schultze earned a PhD from the Institute of Communications Research at the University of Illinois in Urbana–Champaign and taught at Drake University before joining the faculty at Calvin College, where he served as the Arthur H. DeKruyter Chair and a Professor of Communication Arts and Sciences. He received the Presidential Award for Exemplary Teaching in 2000. He is Professor of Communication Emeritus at Calvin College.

Professor Schultze is an honorary Distinguished University Professor of Communication at Spring Arbor University, where he also serves as a visiting professor. He has been a Visiting Distinguished Scholar of Communication at Taylor University and frequent visiting professor at Regent College in Vancouver, BC. He leads master-teaching and book-writing workshops for colleges and universities.

Dr. Schultze has consulted on communication projects for many nonprofit and for-profit organizations. He mentors professionals about their interpersonal (person-to-person), and public communication, including their public speaking. He also conducts communication workshops for employees of small to large organizations.

He has been involved in launching numerous businesses

and nonprofit ventures and continues to invest in and consult with businesses as well as serve on boards of directors.

Dr. Schultze's numerous books include *An Essential Guide to Public Speaking*, *Résumé 101: A Student and Recent-Grad Guide to Crafting Résumés and Cover Letters that Land Jobs*, *An Essential Guide to Interpersonal Communication*, and *Habits of the High-Tech Heart: Living Virtuously in the Information Age*, among others. His books have won six national awards.

His scholarly publications have appeared in several dozen journals, from *Business History Review* to *Qualitative Sociology* and the *Journal of Communication*. He has written over a hundred articles for general-interest periodicals.

Professor Schultze has been quoted in the *The Wall Street Journal*, *Newsweek*, *U.S. News & World Report*, *The Los Angeles Times*, *The New York Times*, *Fortune*, the *Chicago Tribune*, *USA Today*, and many more media. He has been interviewed by CNN, CBS, NBC, ABC, NPR, and numerous radio and television stations, websites, blogs, and podcasts.

Dr. Schultze and his wife, a hospice chaplain, reside in Grand Rapids, Michigan.

Follow his blog posts and publications, subscribe to his free email blog, and download discussion materials for use with this book—all at www.quentinschultze.com. He is on Twitter at #quentinschultze.